Praise for Majendi Jarrett

and the Books in The Complete Loss and Grief Series

"A very hard read but well done. Great effort. Will inspire a lot of people."
—H. Mitchell

"It is very honest and raw. I could not stop reading it until I finished."
—J. Ansong

"It certainly makes compelling reading; you've done exceedingly well."
—Z. Johnson

"It is a good account of Marley's life and I like the way you aligned your thoughts, so you get a complete picture of events." —J. Joyann

"A moving tale of teenage anguish and how a tragic event inspired a grieving family." —S. Lockyer

THE COMPLETE LOSS AND GRIEF SERIES

MARLEY'S MEMOIR, LIVING WITHOUT MARLEY, and HE CARES

MAJENDI JARRETT

Introduction copyright © 2025 by Majendi Jarrett.

Marley's Memoir copyright © 2022 by Majendi Jarrett. Originally published by WestBow Press.

Living Without Marley copyright © 2023 by Majendi Jarrett. Originally published by New Generation Publishing.

He Cares copyright © 2025 by Majendi Jarrett; foreword copyright © 2025 by Alan West.

All rights reserved.

ISBN 978-1-0685524-3-4 (hardcover)

ISBN 978-1-0685524-5-8 (paperback)

ISBN 978-1-0685524-4-1 (ebook)

No part of this book may be used or reproduced by any means, graphic, electronic, or mechanical, including photocopying, recording, taping, or by any information storage retrieval systems without the written permission of the author, except in the case of brief written quotations embodied in critical articles and reviews.

This book is a work of nonfiction. Unless otherwise noted, the author and the publisher make no explicit guarantees as to the accuracy of the information contained in this book and in some cases, names of people and places have been altered to protect their privacy.

Scripture quotations are taken from *The Amplified Bible*, © 1965, 2015, by The Lockman Foundation.

Cover design: Jonathan Hahn

Typesetting: Allison Felus

Printed worldwide through Ingram.

I want to thank my Heavenly Father for giving me the inspiration and the strength to write these books and the desire to put them in a trilogy. A lot of people ask where I get my strength from, and I know that if it were not for Jesus I would not have been able to do all I have done since December 2020.

"I can do all things [which He has called me to do] through Him who strengthens *and* empowers me [to fulfill His purpose—I am self-sufficient in Christ's sufficiency; I am ready for anything and equal to anything through Him who infuses me with inner strength and confident peace.]" Philippians 4:13

Contents

Acknowledgments	ix
Introduction	1
Marley's Memoir	3
Living Without Marley	135
He Cares	231
About the Author	337

Acknowledgments

A very massive thank-you to Allison Felus my editor and coach who has been very instrumental in the production of this trilogy. You have been a great support and given me guidance to make this happen.

A big thank-you to my family and friends who have supported me throughout this journey.

Introduction

I started writing my first book, *Marley's Memoir*, in 2019 not knowing what the ending would be. After publishing it in 2022 and seeing the impact it had with my readers, I was inspired to write the second book, *Living Without Marley*, which gave a voice to the other key family members involved. *Living Without Marley* was published in 2023, and then I got the inspiration to write the third book, which would focus on other significant losses I had had leading up to December 2020. In 2024 I wrote the third book, *He Cares*, and whilst I was writing this final book, I had the inspiration to compile the loss and grief series as a complete trilogy.

For anyone reading my books for the first time, this trilogy makes it easy to get all three titles collected in one volume. For anyone who already has my first book, *Marley's Memoir*, but may not have the second or third, this is an opportunity to gift the first book to someone else and get the full trilogy for your bookshelf.

Marley's Memoir

The Journey to an Irreversible Action and the Aftermath

I dedicate this book to my son, Marley Asher Adeshino Prescott. I would rather have had the eighteen years with you than nothing at all and without you I would not have written this book.

Marley Asher Adeshino Prescott on the beach of Tokeh Village

Contents

Acknowledgments...7

Introduction...9

Part I—In Marley's View

Prologue...13

1 School Days...15

2 A Bottle or Two...18

3 Outed 1...21

4 Holiday in Gambia...25

5 Friends and Private Tutor...28

6 Early School Years...31

7 Enjoying Life...34

8 Allergy and Orlando...38

9 Life in Church...42

10 Something about December...46

11 Paperboy...49

12 No More School...54

13 Who Wants Therapy?...59

14 Outed 2...62

15 Moving Out?...67

16 Is There Something about December?...71

Part II—The Aftermath

Prologue...79

1 Family Life...83

2 Can We Celebrate, Please?...87

3 Never Saw This Coming...92

4 Breaking the News...98

5 Surrounded by Love...103

6 Staying Strong...110

7 Difficult Days...114

8 Hope Amid Pain...118

9 Being Comforted...123

10 Be Encouraged...126

11 Bonus Chapter: Two Aunties...129

"Marley's Song" by M. Grant...133

Acknowledgments

I am grateful to my friends and family for supporting me and encouraging me to write this book. I thank God for everyone who has covered me in prayer and read the first and second drafts, as well as those who have been part of the editing process. I really appreciate all the time and effort you have put into bringing this book to publication. You know who you are, and I am internally grateful for your encouragement and belief in me.

Finally, I would like to give recognition to Levi Lusko's *Through the Eyes of a Lion*, which encouraged me to share my innermost feelings as I could resonate on so many levels when I read his book.

INTRODUCTION

Since I was a little girl growing up, I loved reading. I loved writing essays and doing reading comprehension in school. I loved sharing about what I did on vacation or an interesting place I had visited.

This book started because I wanted to capture what was happening at the time. I wanted to document the weekly interactions with Marley, as at the time I thought this was teenage hormones that he would outgrow. I thought a good way of doing this was to write a book that I would give to Marley when he was older.

Although I always had a desire to write, this was not the book I had in mind. So, when I started this book, especially the chapters in Marley's voice, it wasn't intended for publication until the event that took place in December 2020. I realised others could benefit from what Marley experienced as he tried to navigate anxiety, social awkwardness, and depression. It took a lot of nudging from unlikely sources to take the first steps to finish the book. Then there was a lot of soul searching before I finally took the steps to complete the process of publishing the book.

Marley always sent me voicemail, as it was an easy way to express himself without interruption; sometimes it was how he felt, especially when there had been an argument and he had been unpleasant. Other times he used it to share his point of view on previous conversations in case he forgot, especially if I was away on business travel. He sent voicemails on WhatsApp or text messages, usually with an apology and to give some insight into how he was feeling.

After his demise, when I accessed his phone, I was able to see messages he had sent to online friends and also what he had captured in his mobile notepad. These and the many conversations we had over the years provided the material for his perspective in part two.

Watch out for *Living Without Marley*, which is the sequel to *Marley's Memoir*.

Part I: In Marley's View

Prologue

My name is Marley Asher Adeshino Prescott, born on 3 December 2002.

"So cute," I heard my dad say, admiring my one-day-old self. So many eyes peered at me.

"He's a beautiful baby. He has such a small mouth; I hope he'll be able to latch on to the nipple."

These were all the lovely things that were being said about me two hours after my long-awaited arrival into this world. Well, I say long awaited—I was only two weeks over the due date, but to my mum and dad it felt like a long time.

I was loved and I felt it. I only had to cry for two seconds, and my big brother would be hovering over my carrycot, cooing at me with wide eyes.

"What's wrong, baby brother?" he would ask. "Are you hungry? Have you wet your nappy? Do you want to be picked up?"

My mum would come rushing from the kitchen to the living room. "What did you do to him? Did you try to pick him up?"

My mum would pick me up and I would stop crying. She would check my diaper to see if I was wet or had done a poo. If all was OK, she would check the clock to see what the time was and whether I was close to my next feed.

She seemed to know exactly what I needed: attention. She would get a toy and ask my big brother to play with me so she could finish cooking dinner before my dad got home. I was loved and I felt it.

When dad got home, he would pick me up and stare at me. A few days after my birth, I think he was still wondering how he could have produced such a beautiful baby with such a small mouth that could hardly latch on to the nipple to get enough milk when he was hungry.

"How is my ragamuffin?" he would ask.

Of course he knew I couldn't answer. I was only a few days old; I was trying to make sense of all the different noises, sounds, smells, and touches. I was still coming to terms with this new world. I was no longer in my mother's womb.

I had some work to do if my diaper needed changing or if I wanted some food, as, of course, I was no longer connected by the umbilical cord to an unlimited supply of nourishment.

I was loved and I felt it.

1

School Days

A month after my 15th birthday, I was back at school after the Christmas holidays. I found it hard to adjust to going back because I had to face my peers at school. Meeting new people, no matter their age, was difficult for me. There was something about people staring at me, as if they could see into my thoughts or were making judgments about me.

I'd been trying to fit in at that school for four years, and still it was a struggle because I had no one I could call a friend. I had been let down so many times, and you would think I would have given up.

But no—I still had hopes that maybe, just maybe, someone would move from another school at the start of this term, connect with me, and become my friend. Children from families who had relocated to our area regularly joined my school. Maybe one would be the person I could hang out with during breaks, at lunchtime, and even after school. Yes, I still had some dwindling hopes of having a friend after four years of attending this secondary school.

Usually, if it got to lunchtime on the first day of term and I hadn't connected with any of the newcomers, my hopes of making new friends would disappear. I would conclude that it was not to be, and my time at school would be the same old pattern again this term. I needed something to get me through these first days of school after the holidays.

It was Mum's habit to ask me how my day had been when I got home. This particular day was no different. "How was school today?" she asked.

I grunted something at her with a scowl on my face because when I got home, the last thing I wanted to be reminded of was school.

I wanted to forget about the teachers moving me from seat to seat when I did nothing to warrant it.

I wanted to forget about the kids who I thought were looking at me as if I was weird because I had no one to hang out with at breaks and lunch.

I wanted to forget about all the different subjects that were causing confusion in my mind.

It was hard to smile and give a fake answer to Mum. So I repeated what I'd been saying for four years. "You know exactly how school was—the same as it has been every day I go to that school. Bad. Every day is bad. This is the reason I've repeatedly asked you to move me to another school."

I stomped off to my room before she could respond, as it would be the same response she always gave: "It was too late to move you to another school; your GCSE exams are in just over twelve months, and it would unsettle you."

Blah, blah, blah.

"Who cares about GCSEs and exams?" I replied. Not me. I had bigger problems to sort out.

I reached my room and slammed the door. I knew I would be left alone for at least the next two hours or so while she still worked. She worked from home when she wasn't traveling to other countries for her job.

I sneaked downstairs and reached for my secret bottle of lager that was chilling in the fridge. No one had caught on yet that the bottles of lager were disappearing. I could drink in peace and shut out my immediate problems of school, my lack of friends, and my parents moaning at me all the time. I'd probably fall asleep and wake up with a headache, but hey ho, at least I would have blanked things from my mind for a while and temporarily paused my nonstop thoughts about how I ended up with no friends.

I finished my lager thinking about what my life would be like if I had some friends—well, at least one—and with this in my mind, I fell into a dreamless sleep.

2

A Bottle or Two

I woke up suddenly, not knowing what had interrupted my sleep. Then I heard Mum saying, "Don't you want dinner? You've been sleeping since you came home from school, and it's now seven o'clock."

I had a piercing headache, and while I was still in that waking haze, I wondered what had caused it. Then I became fully awake and wondered if the bottle of lager was in view for her to see, having just realized she was in my room.

I looked around and didn't see any evidence of my drinking spree. Phew! That was lucky; I must have hidden the evidence. I grunted something to get her to leave and moaned that I had a headache. Little did she know that my headache was due to the lager I had drunk to numb the feelings of emptiness I had because of my lack of friends.

I managed to get her to leave, mumbling that I would be down soon for dinner. The pain in my head felt worse. I really needed some painkillers. I regretted drinking. I was now dealing with the aftereffects, and it wasn't pleasant. The relief from not thinking about my loneliness was only temporary. Now I had all those thoughts back in full force, along with a piercing headache and all the worry of someone finding out that I had been drinking. I needed to wash my mouth out and get some pain relief.

After rinsing my mouth to get rid of the alcohol smell, I searched for some gum and headed downstairs.

I checked what was for dinner and asked if I could have some paracetamol. As usual, she told me to have some dinner, which would get rid of the headache. In her opinion, I was too quick to take medication at the slightest hint of pain. I thought better than to argue with her, as I was hungry anyway and speaking only made my head hurt.

I had my dinner of pasta and mince, typical on Tuesdays. I knew exactly what the menu for each day would be, as Mum was predictable in that sense. Leftover Sunday dinner was always on the menu for Monday, and for some reason, pasta and mince was always on Tuesday, which I didn't mind, as I loved pasta. There was some sort of chicken dish with rice on Wednesday and beef on Thursday, while anything goes on Friday.

I loved Fridays for several reasons. Firstly, it was the end of the school week, and secondly, it was the day I could choose my meal; basically, I'd rummage in the freezer for pizza or chips and sausage, which I could put in the oven. The third reason I liked Friday was because I could stay up late on the computer, animating or playing games. I loved it. There was no pressure to go to bed since the next day was Saturday.

My head still hurt after dinner, so I approached her again for the elusive paracetamol. If she hadn't hidden the box, I would have helped myself as I had done in the past. I didn't have a high threshold for pain.

"Mum, could I have two paracetamols? I still have a headache," I said.

She looked at me and told me to go ask my dad. I hated asking him for anything; it was always a longer process than asking Mum.

"Dad won't know where the paracetamol is. Could you please get it?" I put on a sad face to get some sympathy. It worked, and she got me the medication.

I was glad. Soon I would be able to get rid of this headache. But if she only knew what was causing my headache, there would be an outrage. I made sure to get rid of the empty lager bottles before the cleaner came the following week. I didn't want her to find them when she cleaned my room.

That was my thinking, anyway. I didn't expect that by the end of the week I would be outed.

3

OUTED 1

Friday had finally arrived; it was like a long-awaited friend. Because it was the end of the school week, junk food, such as pizza, chips, and sausage—or fish—awaited me when I got home. I pedalled fast after school to rush home.

I got home and noticed that my older brother was inside. I wondered what the occasion was before realizing that he had been home the day before too, because he had celebrated his birthday earlier in the week. He had a few days off work.

I quickly said hello to everyone and rushed off to my room, my haven.

The rest of the afternoon flew by. I decided to have pizza and some oven chips. I made my way downstairs after being on the Xbox for a while.

After having dinner, I was back in my room playing on my phone. Mom knocked on my door and came in. She always entered before I could tell her to come in. I guess she thought she didn't need my permission, and I always wondered why she bothered knocking anyway.

She took a seat on the chair where I usually sit when playing my Xbox and said, "You've drunk almost the whole box of lager that your brother received as a Christmas present from work. I want to know why."

I was stunned. I looked at her with a little smirk on my face. For some unknown reason I always had a smirk on my face no matter how serious the conversation I was having with my family. This usually angered them—they thought I didn't realise the seriousness of the discussion.

This evening was no exception. Mum raised her voice, getting angry. She told me it was illegal at my age to be drinking and asked again why I had drank almost a full box of lager.

All I could think to tell her was that since I didn't get any pocket money and I had a craving for fizzy drinks, this was the reason for my lager drinking. It was basically to satisfy my craving for fizz. I withheld all the other reasons, such as wanting to forget how alone I felt because I didn't have any friends, because I knew this would lead to discussions that I didn't want to have on this occasion.

To my surprise, all her anger seemed to evaporate. "Is that the only reason?"

"Yes," I said to close the matter. I would use this excuse and stick to it, because anything else would cause her to lose sympathy for me.

She said she'd make a deal with me to provide one can of fizzy drink every day to satisfy my craving as long as I promised that I wouldn't touch any more alcoholic drinks without her permission. She said she was aware that it wasn't only the bottles of lager that I had drunk but that I had helped myself to unfinished bottles of Cockspur, a rum from Barbados, and Martini, which were in the cupboard. I had lost count of the different bottles I had reached for in my moments of desperation.

Listening to her go on about the dangers of what I had done slowly brought it home to me that my actions had really disappointed her.

I had to do better. I promised I wouldn't touch any more alcohol. The fact that she had hidden whatever was left made it easy to keep the promise anyway. She had also promised to give me a can of fizzy drink, so if anything, I should be OK. But then I realised it wasn't over, because I knew I had to face my dad and brother.

"Does everyone know about this?" I asked.

"Yes," she responded, "but I told them to wait until I had spoken to you."

In my shock I had forgotten to ask these questions at the start. For some reason her answer made me really angry. I pictured them having full knowledge of what I had done, discussing it whilst I was at school, and greeting me as normal when I got home, even though they knew I had drunk the alcohol. I told her I would have preferred it if everyone had jumped on me as soon as I came through the door rather than keep me in the dark until now. It felt like they had been pretending that everything was OK.

It was Mum's turn to be stunned. She couldn't understand why I was angry. As she had said, she didn't want my dad and brother to jump on me as soon as I came home from school, because she knew how hard school was for me.

I was fuming and shouted at her. She couldn't understand how I felt, having been in this cocoon of comfort for several hours thinking no one knew what I had done, only to find out how wrong I was.

After she left, I immediately sought out my brother to lash out at him in anger. I'd forgotten that I was in the wrong.

He was ready for me. He let loose his anger at me for drinking almost all the lager he had received as a Christmas present. He told me that, as usual, I had got off lightly with Mum promising me fizzy drinks every day. I was oblivious as to how wrong my anger was considering what I had done. I felt justified in believing that my family had betrayed me, which led to my false sense that I was the victim of injustice.

My dad soon joined in the heated discussion, which didn't help matters. He was angry, and I was fuming, and we both had raised voices. Mum intervened by asking me to go to my room. I consented because I didn't want her to take away my cans of fizzy drink. I had let off some steam and could retreat to my room to play my Xbox. It was only Friday, and I wasn't looking forward to the rest of the evening. At least there would be one less person to contend with. My brother was going away with his friends to celebrate his birthday.

4

HOLIDAY IN GAMBIA

Looking back to the previous weekend, as much as I had dreaded constant references to the revelations of Friday night, it turned out to be nothing like that. Apart from a few comments here and there from my dad, which I ignored, all was back to normal for me.

I had come out of the situation with a better deal; getting one can of fizzy drink a day was something I hadn't expected, but I was happy about it.

School continued as normal—if you can call it that. There was nothing normal about it, but I was slowly coming to the realisation that there was nothing I could change. I would soon be leaving the school environment in a matter of months.

I was also looking forward to the Easter break as we were going on holiday to Gambia, a country in West Africa close to Sierra Leone, where my mum is from.

My auntie, who had looked after me when I was a baby, was also joining us in Gambia for the weeklong holiday. It had been two years since she left England to return to Sierra Leone for her daughter's wedding. I was looking forward to seeing her again.

Our time in Gambia was an eye opener. This was the first time I was faced with children my age and younger who had far less than I had. All the issues with school and lack of friends seemed to fade away in light of the abject poverty in which some of the children lived.

We also visited historical sites where captured slaves had been detained before being shipped to America and the Caribbean. I reflected on the suffering my ancestors had faced. It was mind-blowing seeing the cells and chains and hearing the guide narrate horrific stories of how some of these people met their deaths if they weren't strong or fit enough for the life that awaited them in their new destination.

I wasn't exactly empathetic. I had realised that I didn't feel strong emotions over the pain and suffering of others. Don't get me wrong; I wasn't heartless. But on this occasion, after hearing all these sad stories and seeing the evidence, I felt sorry for these people, and maybe because I had felt so lonely, I could relate to some of the despair and agony they had faced. I was moved to give away some of my spending money to the young boys and girls who were following us and begging for anything that we had. I gave away the sweets I had and was amazed at the jostling and fighting by more than twenty children who wanted them.

It made me think about the privileges I had. I was born into a family that had more than enough and didn't want for basic human needs. I had taken it for granted.

When I reflect on our holiday in Gambia, I know that I returned to England with some good feelings. I was a bit more appreciative and grateful for the life I had, even though it wasn't perfect. The good thing was that

I still had some days of holiday before returning to school. I focused on playing Xbox live online and teaching myself animation. I was determined to complete my first video.

Around this time, Mum was planning a party for her 50th birthday, and the holiday to Gambia had been part of the year-long celebrations she had in mind. She asked me to put together a slideshow of the memorable events of the last twelve months and said that I could use this opportunity to launch my YouTube channel. I said I would think about it, but not because I didn't want to do it. I didn't want to be in the spotlight. Having all eyes on me was something I shied away from.

In the end, she asked my brother to do it since I kept telling her I would think about it. But I never took steps to do anything about it, and the day was fast approaching.

5

FRIENDS AND PRIVATE TUTOR

In the weeks leading up to summer vacation, I found out that someone who was the closest I came to calling a friend was leaving the area because his parents had got a new job about two hundred miles north.

It's a funny thing when you realise you'll no longer have what you had. Suddenly you realise how much you'll miss it. The thought of this person moving—someone I hadn't realised was my only friend—was devastating. It's not that we were in the habit of hanging out after school on a regular basis, but I suddenly realised I wouldn't have that opportunity anymore.

I reached out to another boy who was a year below me at school. He was keen to hang out with me after school. For the first time in years, I felt that I had someone I could chill out with … especially when I realised he had access to alcohol and weed.

I was keen to hang out after school, and because I'd been whinging for so long that I didn't have any friends, Mum was quick to say yes when I told her I'd be hanging out with some friends in the park and playing football. Little did she know what I was up to.

It was the much longed-for relief I was looking for: To be out of my room, not thinking about my sad situation of having no friends. I could forget my issues with the help of alcohol and weed whilst hanging out with my so-called friend. I say so-called because deep down, I knew it wouldn't last. He was from a different culture and younger than me, and I guessed that sooner or later his parents wouldn't want him hanging out with me. But while it lasted, I would make good use of the opportunity.

I was drowning my thoughts in alcohol and getting small bottles of vodka that I could smuggle into the house, which I could have when my thoughts tried to get the better of me. I didn't realise that this wasn't the way to deal with my problems, but I couldn't help myself.

Before the start of the new term, my so-called friend had been grounded by his older brother, who told him not to hang out with me; he thought I was a bad influence. Little did he know his brother was the bad influence.

This made me dread the start of the new school term and my final year. I had nothing to look forward to. I put renewed pressure on Mum for a transfer, although there was zero chance of this happening. The previous attempt had been unsuccessful.

Mum secured a private tutor for maths and English but soon realised my efforts should be focused on maths. I was so far behind the syllabus compared to where I should be. I tried to give time and effort to mathematics, but there was too much going on in my head that I couldn't understand. What was the point of trying to explain it to others? All the homework I was given by my private tutor was untouched until the next time we met, and this was really annoying for her. My mind wandered, so I couldn't focus on practising the stuff we had studied when I was on my own. I really tried to concentrate and give attention to it. Mum kept reminding me how much it cost to have a private tutor twice a week.

Despite my efforts appearing minimal to others, I thought I was doing a lot. No one knew what I was going through day in, day out, just dealing with all the thoughts in my head.

After several lessons of untouched homework, my tutor finally gave up. She told Mum that it was a waste of time; I just wasn't interested. Every piece of homework she gave me I hadn't done, and whatever we did during the previous lesson she would have to go through all over again.

In her opinion it was a waste of money. It would be better to stop now than to waste more money on private tutoring. Even though she was getting paid, at the end of the day I would have nothing to show for it. I guess she was also concerned about her reputation. She didn't want to get a review that indicated she spent a year tutoring me and I still didn't get a good grade in my GCSE in mathematics.

In a way I was happy, but at the same time I wasn't. I knew Mum would be upset and angry about how much she had spent on private tuition, especially if I didn't get the grades in my forthcoming examination.

6

Early School Years

Sometimes I wonder how I ended up the way I am—wanting friends but not having any, or pushing away people who had tried to befriend me because they weren't meeting my expectations of what a friend should be.

I think I was happy for the first ten years of my life. I never had to deal with staying at different houses with different child minders, which other young children experienced at an early age. My parents had invited a close family friend from Africa, the auntie who reunited with us on our Gambian holiday, to live with us. She came over when I was a baby to look after me and my brother, since my parents worked full time.

My brother and I were never shuffled from one house to another after school or during school holidays. My auntie took me to playgroup when I was little since Mum didn't want me to go to nursery until I could go to preschool. Later, in my teens, I had asked her if the reason I was finding it hard to make friends was because I hadn't gone to nursery. I had grown up being more comfortable on my own.

She disagreed, saying that I had an older brother. Although he was about three years older than me and there wasn't much of an age gap between us, I had always preferred playing on my own. I would play for hours with my toys because sometimes what I wanted to do was different to what my brother wanted to do. This led to me being quite content to play by myself. Even when I did make friends at preschool, I could easily leave them whilst I went to another room to play by myself.

I knew my auntie might have thought that was odd, but to me it was fine. That gave my brother the freedom to do what he wanted while I had the freedom to do what I wanted. That was the way I saw it, and many, including Mum, didn't agree with me, but it was OK.

Even when we went on holiday for the first time, I only wanted to play or hang out with my brother. But being the social butterfly he was, there were always other children competing for his attention. I had realised at that early age that I wasn't going to compete and would therefore leave him with his new friends and play by myself.

Nevertheless, whether it was from spending long days alone with my auntie whilst my parents went to work and my brother went to school, I had developed the art of living within my head. I expressed myself through my Lego toys.

When I started preschool, boys and girls wanted to be my friends, but I was overwhelmed and shied away.

One girl wouldn't give up and pulled me into her circle of friends. After school, we happily walked along with my auntie and her mum when they picked us up from school. It was a bag of mixed emotions: lovely on one hand that someone wasn't put off by my awkward and shy disposition, but on the other hand, I felt a bit intimidated. I couldn't say no when she pulled me along during playtime or heading home after school.

Eventually, I was bold enough to break away from her circle of girls and make my own friends. I probably learnt a thing or two from her; I became the bold one in my newly found group of three friends. I dictated what games we played and basically used the tricks I had learnt from my first girlfriend, as I liked to call her. I moved from preschool into the first year of school with this group. I made sure no one could break our tight group of three. I kept out any other boys or girls who tried to join us. I was happy, but I didn't realise it wasn't going to last beyond lower school.

7

Enjoying Life

The first ten years of my life were the happiest. I was the leader of a close circle of friends. I dictated what we did at school and after school. My closest friend stayed at my house until his parents picked him up after work.

Shyness aside, I was in a happy place. I could play on my own if that was the mood I was in, or I could play with my close friend or my brother. My brother also had a close friend who was the son of one of my mum's closest friends. We went places together as a trio with our parents.

Every half-term holiday or during the main school holidays, we went to the cinema to watch the latest animated movies. We got popcorn and other snacks and munched our way through the movies. I watched movies such as *Shrek*, *The Incredibles*, *Wreck-It Ralph*, *Up*, and many others. We also rented movies on video or DVD, and they were the last thing we watched before going to bed.

My brother and I had bunkbeds. I had the bottom bunk until he got bigger, and then we swapped. Those were good days as we fought and made up. Mainly we argued over what to watch. I usually won, because as soon as Mum heard us, she took my side because I was younger. She told my brother to look after me and give me the first choice, and then we watched what he wanted.

It was fun because we had our own telly and DVD player, so we could control what we watched. Our parents hardly bothered us when we said goodnight and went to bed. During those nights we also sneaked biscuits and crisps into our bedroom by hiding them in our pants when going upstairs.

Most of the time we got away with it, but sometimes I would give away that something was in my pants because I walked funny. Mum asked why I was walking funny and then discovered the biscuits or other snacks. I would lose my snacks and get told off. By then we would already have brushed our teeth, which meant no more food or drinks.

As we got older, we sneaked movies from our parents' collection, which we weren't allowed to watch. But there was something about watching a forbidden movie that we couldn't resist. On occasions, we had my brother's friend for a sleepover, and we all had so much fun. Whilst this friend was the same age as my brother, he treated me as if I was their age We wrestled and tumbled about, and sometimes when it got too noisy, my dad would tell us off.

On other occasions we went to the park to play football, have fun on the slides, or ride our bikes. Other times we went on trips to theme parks or animal farms for the whole day.

Other times, my school friend's parents asked Mum and Dad if I could join them on a family trip. On such an occasion we went to Winter Wonderland, and I ate a nice juicy hotdog. That was a memorable day. Another time we went to Thorpe Park, and I was able to go on most of the rides because I met the height requirement.

One of the highlights of those early years was going away on my first holiday to Tunisia with my family, my close friend, and his family. I was a baby or very young on previous holidays and couldn't remember what had gone on. So, when Mum arranged with my friend's mum that we should all go on holiday to Tunisia, I was very excited. We arrived in Tunisia very late after flying from Birmingham airport.

My brother and I had our own room with ensuite, and it made us feel grown up, although there was a connecting door to our parents' room. We spent a lot of time in the pool, and although I wasn't a good swimmer, I had floaters, which made me feel protected and safe.

Sometimes during the day there were activities led by the entertainment team. We could participate or we could just sit on our loungers and enjoy the show. On other occasions, we went on a day trip organised by the hotel. On one of these trips, my dad and I rode a camel. Although it was very smelly, the experience of being so far from the ground on an animal I had only seen on telly was thrilling.

What I enjoyed most on this particular holiday were the evenings when we would have a change of clothes for dinner, and I could choose what I wanted to eat and had access to unlimited fizzy drinks since we had wristbands indicating that we were part of an all-inclusive package.

After dinner we either went for a walk to explore the surrounding area or stayed at the hotel to watch an evening show. Either option was fine by me; it meant we were staying out late and not going to bed early, which was the norm when we were at home.

We discovered I was allergic to one of the ingredients in the sun lotion Mum had bought for us to use. It was about the third day of our holiday when I woke up with one side of my face really puffed up. My mum and dad were quite concerned and got a doctor to examine me. I was prescribed some medication to fight the allergic reaction, and over the coming day or two the puffiness slowly reduced. Once the puffiness disappeared, I was back to spending a lot of time in the pool—without sun cream.

We already knew my brother and I were allergic to nuts, but we had never been tested, so getting this reaction from the sun lotion was something else to worry about.

It was an enjoyable holiday, and one I remembered for a long time. Finally, I could go back to school, tell my friends all about it, and I was able to write in my English class about what I had done whilst on holiday.

8

Allergy and Orlando

Due to the allergic reaction I had in Tunisia, Mum decided to get me tested for allergies. Unfortunately, before the appointment I had another incident whilst away on an overnight school trip. I hadn't taken any sun lotion with me as Mum knew that I had reacted to it. But a teacher decided to put sun cream on me, and I immediately reacted to it with the same puffiness on one side of my face.

The teacher was extremely alarmed and made a phone call to Mum. I was immediately sent back home with a teacher, and that was the first and last overnight trip I did during my time at school. I hated the unnecessary focus on me and the attention from all the teachers. If Mum was having any doubt about me being tested, this incident confirmed that she needed to get it done.

I was taken to the doctor, who referred me to the hospital. My mum was asked to prepare different cookies following a recipe sent by the hospital. Each cookie had a different type of nut in it, and this tested my reaction. I was a bit concerned because on the odd occasion when we'd been to parties and I'd had a bite of food containing some type of nut, my lips would become swollen whilst my throat got very scratchy. My mum assured me that since I would be tasting them in a controlled environment in the hospital, I'd be fine.

When we arrived at hospital, I thought it would be over quickly. I had visions of finishing early and getting home to play my games. Unfortunately, it was almost an all-day event. Each cookie with the different type of nut was tested individually. Some I had to have a little bite and then be observed. With others the cookie was put on my skin and any reaction noted. I was pleasantly surprised that I wasn't allergic to almonds or hazelnuts. I had a strong reaction to peanuts, which wasn't a surprise at all. I also had a strong allergy to Brazil, cashew, and pistachio nuts.

I had one up on my brother. I could eat any chocolates with almonds or hazelnuts in them without fear of an allergic reaction, but because he hadn't been tested, he had to stay away from all nuts.

Not too long after my testing, Mum told me our next holiday would be in Orlando, Florida. I'd been asking for this trip for what seemed like forever. Although I enjoyed the holiday to Tunisia, the one I enjoyed the most was in Orlando.

In the summer of 2012, we went to Orlando. My mum always said I was fearless. I was raring to go on roller coasters, no matter how high or scary they were. I loved the adrenaline rush.

I counted down the days to our holiday in Orlando. We had to go to Gatwick the day before as the flight was leaving quite early in the morning, and since we were taking the train, we didn't want to risk missing our flight.

We were also travelling with another family of six, which included four boys—three of whom were around the same age as me. I thought it might be good to have young people to talk to instead of strangers.

The hotel wasn't the same as the one we had in Tunisia. It wasn't all-inclusive. My mum said the holiday was expensive as we were there for about ten days, so we had to go for a cheaper hotel. I didn't mind as long as we had the passes for all the rides. There was also a pool at the hotel where we spent time cooling off when it was too hot.

On the first day we went to Walt Disney World, and I was a bit disappointed. It wasn't what I was expecting. It was more for little kids, but our parents thought we should experience all that we had paid for, so I had no choice but to put up with this kiddie stuff until we could go to the bigger rides. I was looking forward to Universal Studios Hollywood.

Over the next ten days we visited all the famous theme parks I had heard so much about from kids in school who had already been on holiday to Florida. I was able to go on most of the rides because I met the height requirements. There were some rides my brother couldn't go on because he suffers from motion sickness, but for me, the higher and faster the experience, the better it was.

We also had some trips to the shopping mall when Mum said to choose some trainers, T-shirts, and any souvenirs we wanted to take back with us. We attended some shows and had dinner at different restaurants, and I met one of my cousins who I had never met before because she lived in Florida with her husband. They joined us for drinks one evening at our hotel.

There were other holidays we went on during the next six years, but none was more enjoyable than our Orlando holiday.

9

LIFE IN CHURCH

Mum was very spiritual, and every Sunday we went to church, although Dad only came on special occasions, such as Christmas, Father's Day, or Easter. From a young age I remember going to Little and Loud, which was Sunday school for young children. It would be wrong to say I didn't like it, but I used to cry, and sometimes the Sunday school teacher would get Mum from the service. It was more a case of not wanting to be amongst other children that I didn't know. I wanted to be with Mum and my auntie, and I didn't want to get to know other children. It would have been better if I was left on my own to play with the toys and didn't have to mix with the others. Gradually, as I got older, I became more settled but still wouldn't say much at Sunday school.

One of my Sunday school teachers, who was a friend of Mum's, would say how quiet I was and always looked out for me, trying to get me to say something or to join in the activities. Around this time, I realised I liked drawing and could get lost sketching different cartoons and pictures. Whenever we had activities that included drawing or something to do with art, I was happy to immerse myself in it. My parents and auntie told me I had a talent, and even my brother told me I was really good. For me it was just something I liked doing and that I could get engrossed in.

Church in those early days was somewhere I went on Sundays because Mum wanted me to go. With time, I used it to get something I had developed a love for: McDonald's. We stopped there to get something for lunch so Mum or my auntie didn't have to prepare something at home. On other occasions we left church later and stopping by McDonald's for lunch became the norm. Mum soon realised it was a way of getting me to go to church.

I had outgrown the younger Sunday school classes but didn't want to go to the over-twelves class. At the same time, I found sitting in church with all the adults boring, so I made excuses not to go to church, especially when my older brother decided he didn't want to go every Sunday but only on special occasions.

I was asked to play Joseph in the Christmas nativity on the Sunday before Christmas. I didn't want to do it—I was nervous about being up on stage and having all those people staring at me—but I accepted. We practiced in Sunday school at first, and Mum was told what the dress code was for the role of Joseph on the day. I think it was two weeks before the Nativity when I caught chickenpox. Whilst it was uncomfortable, I thought it would get me out of the Nativity; someone else could take my place. My mum, on the other hand, wasn't having it. She must have been longing for one of us to be given such a leading role. She got this white stuff to put on my spots. My auntie, who knew all the traditional remedies from

Sierra Leone, put forward some solutions so that I would be ready for my part as Joseph.

I realised I wasn't cut out to be in the limelight. I was uncomfortable with it.

Years later, my brother teased me whenever we saw the girl who had played the part of Mary and said, "There goes your Mary!"

I would get annoyed and say, "She's not my Mary."

I knew I was no actor and preferred to be behind the scenes. As if my stint in a nativity wasn't enough, Mum decided to enrol my brother and me in a Saturday drama school. It seemed she was determined to make an actor out of me. At first it was fun to be out of the house on a Saturday, taking a walk up the road to the drama school, which was about ten minutes from our house.

But it was no longer fun when the drama teacher decided I was to play a part in the production in which my older brother had a starring role. I started dreading going to drama school and told my auntie and Mum I didn't want to do it. I was so stressed out about it that Mum had to speak to the teacher to let her know I was no longer going to be part of it. Again, I realised I didn't like being in the spotlight whilst my brother seemed to love it.

Surprisingly, I didn't have a problem being part of the school Christmas production. During my years at my lower school there were many occasions when I was part of a group performance, and my parents, and sometimes my nan and my auntie, would be invited to school to watch.

My brother and I also attended Friday Night Club at church, but that didn't last long. After a full day of school, I wasn't always in the mood to be around people I didn't know, even though my brother would also be there. One incentive for going to the Friday Night Club was the access to sweets and junk food. Though Mum let us have fizzy drinks or sweets, it was only on special occasions (until later, after the lager incident). I had discovered from an early age when attending friends' birthday parties that I loved anything sugary.

I say "friends" loosely because, in those days, you didn't have to be a close friend. The whole class would be invited to a birthday party because that was the thing to do. If Mum was free and I had some interactions with the birthday boy or girl, then I would attend, but Mum didn't see the point of spending money and effort if I never played with the person who had invited me.

On the occasions when I got an invite to a McDonald's party, of course I would tell Mum that I played with the person during lunchtime just so I could go to McDonald's! I didn't mind going to parties that were held at a local place called Snakes and Ladders; it was a play centre where you could do your own thing.

I wouldn't say I was a loner, but I definitely didn't like to be around too many people. I preferred one or two people. Even when it was my birthday and Mum wanted me to invite friends from school, I preferred just a few from school, the friends I knew outside school, and my cousins.

10

SOMETHING ABOUT DECEMBER

One of my favourite times of the year (apart from the summer holidays) was December. My birthday was at the start of December, and, of course, there were the Christmas holidays, decorating the house, putting up the Christmas tree and lights, and, of course, getting birthday and Christmas presents.

I usually made a list of what I wanted for my birthday and for Christmas. This way Mum knew what was urgent and what could wait until Christmas. I always chose games and games console. I hardly asked for clothes and just wasn't bothered about things like that. In December 2016, the list for my birthday was Dragon Ball Xenoverse 2 video game for Xbox One, WWE 2K17 video game for Xbox, and a graphic/drawing tablet.

For Christmas, the list consisted of a Google Pixel phone, money, and a laptop. I got everything on my birthday list but got other things for Christmas. Mum didn't think I needed an expensive Google phone since I had a reputation for breaking most of the electronics I owned. I didn't get the laptop either because I used the desktop PC in the house. I wanted the convenience of having a laptop that I could take to my bedroom, especially at night. I knew I wouldn't get the money on my list—Mum never gave us money for Christmas (except pocket money, which was rather random, and it was the first thing to go if we did something wrong).

Even when I decided I didn't want to take a packed lunch to school and preferred to buy food at school, she gave me lunch money every day instead of weekly. It was a pain, but there was nothing I could do about it.

After my birthday, the following weekend we put up the Christmas decorations. Mum always asked me to help with the Christmas tree decorations, whilst my brother helped Dad with the lights in the front garden. I asked for some lights in my bedroom window and in the front windows of the house. It was my job to turn the lights on and off when I was younger. I loved seeing the house all lit up in the evening.

When we were younger, my parents took me and my brother to Toys"R"Us during December so we could get a gift for each other. We split up. I usually went with Mum, my brother with Dad. At first I was more concerned with getting something for myself; the store was full of so many things I would have loved to have. Our parents told my brother and me that we needed to think of others and not just about ourselves, but once I got inside, I couldn't think of anything except for what I could get for myself. I'm sure it was a stressful time for our parents, especially the few occasions when I was paired off with my dad.

Eventually something meant to be fun would end up with me in tears because I didn't get what I wanted. I'm glad my behaviour didn't put Mum off. The following year we were back in the store doing it all over again—after convincing Dad that it was worth it.

Another December memory was the smell of Christmas cake being baked in the oven. Every year Mum baked this traditional Christmas cake (which Caribbean people call black cake)—a rich cake prepared with fruits soaked in rum. I think I got a little tipsy eating it! The smell of cinnamon, nutmeg, and vanilla pulled me downstairs. I longed for a taste. I was only given a small piece, but later I helped myself when no one was around.

The smell of the cooked ham and turkey on Christmas Day was one of my favourite times. We usually went to church as a family in the morning. I looked forward to singing "The Twelve Days of Christmas", when all the males in church stood up for the odd numbers and all the women stood up for the even numbers. It was definitely a highlight of Christmas Day before we got home and opened our presents.

11

Paperboy

I can't say exactly when it started, but I know that at the end of 2018 or the beginning of 2019, I was fed up with school. Maybe it wasn't just school though, because I even seemed to have lost the joy I felt when the weekend was approaching. Going to school was a chore, and my GCSEs were starting in May. I was nowhere close to where I should be with my grades, and I was under pressure to do well so I could go to college and study animation, which was the only thing I enjoyed doing these days.

I constantly told Mum I wasn't happy and that every school day was a bad day. I just didn't get any pleasure from being at school. It got so bad that Mum took me to the doctor again to get a referral because I was all over the place. I couldn't help talking back and arguing with anyone who asked me how I was after I got home from school. I knew I was a nightmare, but I couldn't do anything about it.

The doctor told us to get the school to refer me for outside support since I didn't want anyone in school to know my business. I had seen how other children who needed support were ridiculed and I had enough on my plate without adding this too. I was given a letter to take to the person responsible for school pastoral care. This was a task in itself. I didn't want to be seen with this particular teacher; if someone saw me, schoolmates would know and would conclude there was something wrong with me.

On the day I was supposed to meet with pastoral care, Mum kept phoning me. The teacher had given specific instructions as to where and when I should meet her to do the referral, but I hadn't turned up. As much as I wanted to get the referral done, there were too many people around who could see me, so I didn't go.

After two days of Mum pushing me to speak to the teacher, I finally had the meeting with her. She tried to tell me I could receive support in school, but I said I would prefer it to be external. She finally agreed and wrote a letter recommending outside organisations.

I believed this was the end of it, since I now had a piece of paper that said I was suffering from anxiety due to my forthcoming GCSEs. I figured I didn't need to see anyone else in or outside school. My mum was having none of it. She insisted I take the opportunity to address my ongoing issues; daily complaints about school, my lack of friends, inability to maintain friendships, and my growing social anxiety.

I got to the point where it made me really anxious if family and friends were coming round. I didn't want to visit family, and I didn't look forward to family gatherings at our house. I usually felt awkward at any gathering, whether it was close family members or not. I was okay with my immediate family, but with anyone else, it was difficult to socialise.

I would go on about it for days or weeks before the event, especially if I was the last to find out because I spent so much time in my room. I definitely needed professional help although I didn't want it.

After a lot of persuasion, Mum convinced me to take a call from an organisation supporting children and young people with anxiety disorders. I was asked several questions and tried to answer truthfully, although I didn't want to tell them everything I thought and felt. I didn't believe anyone would understand—sometimes conversations with my brother or Mum went round in circles. They didn't understand how or why I felt the way I did. I didn't understand it myself, so how could I explain it to anyone else? I figured if my immediate family couldn't understand me, what were the chances someone who didn't even know me would understand?

After about three or four telephone consultations I was given six sessions to attend at their local office with a dedicated consultant. I wasn't looking forward to it at all. I'm not a talker, especially with someone I don't know.

But just before I started attending these sessions, I had a breakthrough in another area. Since I was 13, I tried to get a job as a paperboy. I regularly spoke to the guy who owned the shop asking him to give me a chance. At first I was below the age requirements, and later, when I was old enough, there were no openings.

I wanted a bit of independence. My brother was working as an apprentice in a local component firm and could buy whatever he wanted. I wanted to earn some pocket money and not be so dependent on my parents for everything

Finally, around the Easter holidays, one of the girls with a regular paper round was going on holiday, and the newsagent asked me if I could cover her for a week. I was so excited; it felt like such a big achievement. My mum was really pleased, although both my parents had reservations about whether I would be able to do it successfully. I wasn't known as an early riser and sometimes ran late for school. This job would mean I had to get up extremely early—earlier than when I got ready for school—to be at the shop to collect the papers and deliver them.

I also had to follow a specific route to ensure that I delivered the papers to the correct houses. I had to shadow the girl before she went on holiday, and it was one of those awkward situations with me not saying much because I didn't know what to say.

On the Saturday morning for my trial, I woke up early, even though I had asked Mum to wake me up. That was just a backup plan in case I overslept.

My trial run was an eye-opener. There were about thirty-six houses on my round to deliver newspapers, and they were scattered all over the area where we lived. I soon realised I needed a bag that would be easily accessible to extract the papers whilst still enabling me to ride my bike. I also needed to remember all the addresses to which I was delivering; putting a paper through the wrong letter box wasn't acceptable.

Mistakes meant deductions from my earnings. I had proper responsibility. It was my first trial job, and I was determined to succeed. I had to prove to my parents and myself that I could do this. I arrived home a little exhausted, trying to work out my plan of action—the following Monday I would have to do this by myself.

On Monday I made mistakes and had some wages deducted because the shop owner had to correct my errors. After a few days it got better, and I understood what I needed to do. This was the beginning of my independence. My trial paper route was successful, and after I finished my GCSEs, the shop owner gave me a permanent round. I was ecstatic. I had a regular income to spend on what I liked and no longer needed to ask my parents for everything.

12

No More School

The excitement of being offered the paper round was short-lived as I soon had to sit my exams, which I was ill-prepared for. I even lacked the motivation to complete tasks for my artwork, which wasn't normal. Art was my thing.

Even though my parents had tried to incentivise me with money if I achieved certain grades, it still didn't push me to do more. I constantly got into trouble with the art teacher. She chased me to bring in my completed work, and in the end, she reached out to Mum, who of course insisted I complete the work that very evening so I could take it into school.

Did I do my best? Definitely not! I was at that point where I needed to get the teacher and Mum off my back, so I quickly did work that would pass as completed and handed it in. If you asked me why I didn't put in the effort, I couldn't give you an answer. But my head definitely wasn't in the right place. This was more evidence that I needed the outside support—which I was resisting.

I started attending the talking therapy sessions after finishing my GCSEs. Around the same time, there was the Leaver's Dance, which I had decided I wouldn't attend. I didn't see the point—I didn't have any friends, and I always felt awkward at such gatherings, so why torture myself? I was happy to receive some money from Mum. She told me she would give me one hundred pounds. It was part of the money she would have spent on me if I had gone to the Leaver's Dance. I kept some of it and used the other half on my favourite junk food.

Finally, I was a school leaver! I no longer had to go to the school I had hated for the last five years. I didn't have to see the people I didn't want to see. I felt I could do what I wanted. I was also aware that I needed to do something to get me out of the house. I still had the paper round, which was a couple of hours early in the morning each day. I needed something where I could interact with people on my own terms at a level that I could manage.

My brother helped me create my CV, and I applied for a lot of summer jobs, one at McDonald's. I wanted to do a job on my own terms. I thought I could apply for any job and then at the interview make it clear I only wanted part-time hours—even if the job was advertised as being full-time. Obviously, this became a big stumbling block.

I was determined to be out of the house, even if it meant volunteering at the local charity shop. I got an application form and was successful in being taken on. I had put on the form that I wanted tasks that involved sorting out the donated items so I would be in the background. I wasn't prepared for any customer-facing. It wasn't my thing. My worst nightmare would be working on the tills and speaking to customers.

The first two days went better than expected. I was in the back room sorting out CDs and DVDs that had been donated. I had limited interaction was people, which was fine by me. The third day didn't go so well. I was told the day before that I would be put on the till so I could cover in case the regular person wasn't in. I dreaded it. I considered stopping altogether. After a pep talk from Mum and my brother I decided to at least try once.

I arrived on the day and was shown what I needed to do. One of the senior volunteers would be with me during my shift. It was difficult for me as my anxiety kicked in. My palms grew sweaty, and my heart pounded as if I was running a hundred metres a minute. I felt stressed and didn't want to do it anymore. Although I had done a session with my support worker, who gave me coping mechanisms and tips to overcome these feelings, I realised I couldn't remember anything I was being shown. I tried, but it was making me miserable, so I stopped volunteering at the charity shop.

Around the same time, I got an interview with McDonald's, but I was beginning to think this wouldn't work. I would be around people all the time and would feel awkward and uncomfortable.

I went to the interview so that my parents and brother wouldn't be annoyed with me for not trying, but I knew deep down that it wasn't a job I would feel comfortable doing. I guess I didn't put a great deal of effort into the interview.

My dad dropped me off in the town centre, but my anxiety was already kicking in just thinking about the interview. I didn't recognise where I was and had to call Mum, who gave me directions. I arrived late to the interview.

I was asked if I was available seven days a week as that was what had been advertised. I told the woman I could only do Friday to Sunday. I didn't get the job. After this I gave up trying to get a summer job.

Soon after, the GCSE results were out, and I didn't get the grades I needed to go to college and study animation. I felt my life spiralling out of my control. If I couldn't get a job at McDonald's or cope with volunteering at the charity shop, what would I do for a living? What would my future look like? These questions kept churning round and round in my head, and I had no answer. I focussed on teaching myself animation and creating videos for my YouTube channel. I saw this as the only way for a future career.

When Mum asked me to retake some of my GCSEs, I told her I didn't need to go to college to be formally trained as I could teach myself.

Around this time, I decided I didn't want to continue with the help I was getting from the support worker. I didn't want to reveal some of the thoughts I was having. I told Mum that I wouldn't attend the last two sessions and used the excuse that the support worker had changed one of the session dates because he was going on vacation.

I was having a constant battle with Mum. She wouldn't let me get away with not attending some sort of studies to try to get back on track. I told her I needed a break until the end of 2019. After all, I was still recovering from all the stress I had dealt with at school.

She agreed but wanted me to attend an animation workshop, which included a week staying at a residential centre and then three weekends of sessions. I was interested, but the idea of being away from home and staying with strangers for a whole week didn't appeal to me.

It's funny that I had now become this antisocial person, when a few years back I was constantly begging Mum to look for an animation club I could attend. This was around the time when I realised that I wasn't into football and had no interest in all the different types of afterschool sport clubs—unlike my brother, who was involved with an under-14s football club at the time.

13

WHO WANTS THERAPY?

It was a cold January morning. We had just landed back in England after seven nights in Freetown, Sierra Leone. I was glad to be back in my own safe space. Seven days of putting on a smiley face had left me with aching face muscles. I could go back to my routine of paper round, animation, Xbox Live games, and online games, such as Habbo, which I enjoyed. No more meeting family members I didn't know and would probably never see again. I felt relieved.

We got home, and Mum was immediately on my back to empty out my suitcase. She had put her stuff and things for other people in it. Whilst taking stuff out, I pulled out the outfit and souvenirs from my auntie, the one who had looked after me from the time I was a baby until I was 12, when she decided to go back to Sierra Leone for her daughter's wedding. I thought about the day we spent with her. It was definitely one of the highlights of my time in Sierra Leone. She always cared about me, and to a certain extent I think I was her favourite. I wondered if I would ever get to see her again. It wasn't as if I made a habit of taking that long journey to Freetown.

I hadn't wanted to go in the first place. The thought of all those people—young and old, ones I knew and didn't know—all in one place and all looking at me filled me with dread. I was protesting for the eleven months before we even had our first jabs that I didn't want to go to Sierra Leone.

I know I caused Mum a lot of stress by being uncooperative about the general preparations for the trip. I couldn't make up my mind what clothes I needed to take. Some were too small, and I only told Mum this a few days before we were due to travel. I was also missing sliders and swimwear. Who can blame me? I didn't want to go, so I was being difficult every step of the way. If she could have seen inside my head, and if she had known the number of times I had to calm myself by taking stuff I had no business taking, she would have left me in England.

She kept saying, "You're having a holiday in a hot sunny place, staying in a hotel on the beach, with all expenses taken care of, and you don't want to go? Who would say no to that?"

If only she knew the thoughts going through my head, she would have cancelled the whole trip and got me to a psychiatrist. Just kidding—it wasn't that bad. She knew I had a serious case of anxiety about being in social gatherings and meeting new people, so of course going to my cousin's wedding would accelerate my anxiety attacks.

Anyway, that was all behind me now. It was a new year, and I was thinking about my future and my future plans. I knew that sooner or later, the topic of retaking my GCSEs or going to college or something would crop up. Just thinking about it depressed me. I had finished school, and here I was with nothing to show for it. My only way out was the animation videos I was creating and uploading to my YouTube channel. I wanted to get more likes and subscribers, but it was moving really slow.

I was becoming the hermit Mum had accused me of becoming, because I was hardly out of my room. Once I returned from my paper round and got breakfast, I retreated into my room and stayed there until evening. I only came out to get dinner. Sometimes Mum would come looking for me, but mostly I was left alone. They knew I would only get annoyed if someone came into my room.

Mum must have picked up something from my behaviour because she told me I needed to speak to someone. She said I was most likely depressed. I probably was, but I wouldn't admit it. I didn't want to speak to anyone. Part of me was afraid I'd spill out the dark thoughts running through my head, and then I might be labelled as troubled or mad or something. How many times had I shared some of my thoughts and then been asked what was wrong with me by one family member or another? I was only saying what was on my mind. I had a telephone appointment, which I knew I needed to accept if I wanted my favourite food. Mum definitely knew how to bribe me. I had no choice. I had to participate in the call, but I also prepared myself for what I would say. I didn't want to give away too much. I had to keep my guard up at all times.

14

OUTED 2

A week later I was diagnosed with mild depression and offered ten counselling sessions with a therapist. I didn't want to attend. I felt it would be like the other support I had experienced in my last year of school. Unless I was prepared to open up and tell them everything that was going on in my head, it would be useless.

My mum, of course, had other ideas. She felt that I needed to speak to someone and told me to take it one session at a time. She sensed my unwillingness to do even one session, let alone ten.

I only attended one session, because then we were in lockdown due to the Covid-19 pandemic. The prime minister had announced that no social interaction was permitted outside our immediate household.

For me, it was the ideal situation. I no longer had to attend family events or visit aunties and uncles. We all had to stay in our own space. I loved it, not realising that it was slowly making me worse. At least when family visited, it forced me to interact, to be social. In this situation I could just stay in my room and only make appearances at mealtimes.

My mum wasn't having it, though. She constantly tried to get me to go out into the garden for family barbecues or al fresco breakfast or something or the other. I was resisting all the way. I became withdrawn, barely spoke to my family unless I wanted something, and was flippant and obnoxious when anyone tried to ask me about anything I had done wrong.

I was also speaking to online contacts, asking opinions about different topics that I felt I couldn't discuss with anyone who knew me. I had withdrawn from my cousins and family friends, so I didn't share how I was feeling with them. My mum continued to try to get me to do more sessions with the therapist. I told her I was all right; I didn't need any more sessions. Sometimes she left me alone, but after a few weeks she would be back on my case. I was irritated, especially when she smelt weed on my clothes, my source of temporary relief, and what I'd been trying to hide came to light.

She was certain I had the weed in my room and insisted I give it to her. She took my laptop, which I had bought with my paper round money.

"Until you give me the weed you have hidden in your room, you won't get your laptop back," she threatened.

I'd underestimated her sense of smell. I realised I needed stronger air freshener to disguise it. I had checked online how to disguise the smell, but obviously it wasn't enough. I was really angry at that point and felt this overwhelming dislike for her. In fact, not just for her, but for my whole family.

"Why are you so against weed? It helps me, and it's only for recreational use," I said.

In the end I gave her the weed to get my laptop back. I knew she would destroy it, but what choice did I have?

The anger I felt later when I thought about what had happened really frightened me. I realised that I could have hit her, and that would have been unforgivable. What was happening to me? It was only weed. I used it to dull the thoughts in my head, and I had bought it with my own money. The laptop was purchased with my paper round money. She had no right to take these things away from me, I reasoned within myself. I was fuming. I needed to put an end to this.

I knew someone had been snooping around my room—one of my lighters was missing. I wanted to call them out, but how would I explain why I was in possession of the lighter? I couldn't, so I let it go and became even more withdrawn. I lacked privacy even in my own home.

I would barely greet Mum because I was still consumed with anger. I didn't speak to my dad, and I hardly said two words to my brother. I felt like they were all against me and I was on my own.

I was constantly doing things that annoyed them. It's not that I was going out of my way to be obnoxious, it was more about me not caring. I would leave things out of the fridge or not clean up after I made a mess. I constantly put food in the oven and retreated to my room until someone shouted for me to come get it, which really annoyed my parents.

When I was being told off for what I had done, I had a habit of walking away whilst Mum or Dad was speaking, and this aggravated the situation even more. I couldn't seem to help myself.

In the midst of all the angst I had against my family, I was especially angry with my dad. Don't ask me why; I couldn't tell you if I tried. Maybe it's because Mum seemed to have more patience with me.

Dad was great at baking. He made really delicious cakes, such as sweet bread, sponge cakes, and other really yummy stuff. I would be in my room and the smell of it would get me downstairs to investigate. Later, when all the goodies were laid out and no one was around, I helped myself. I would later get told off because I had eaten it all without thinking that others might not have had any.

At the same time, I was constantly saying sorry to Mum or texting her with apologies after I'd had time to calm down and reflect on the situation. Deep down I knew I was at fault, but I couldn't help myself.

The incident with the weed could have been a turning point for me. I started thinking how much I needed my independence. I needed my own place where I could do what I wanted. I started working towards what I thought was my freedom.

I told Mum shortly after this weed incident that I didn't want to go to college to do animation but instead wanted to work. I explained that later on maybe I would go to college, but for now I wanted to get out there and earn a living.

One of the agencies I'd reached out to after I finished school wanted to give me a job, but I needed to be 18 to work in a warehouse. I was thinking that as soon as I turned 18 and could get that job, I would move out and get my own place. I hadn't considered all the details of what that meant.

All I was thinking about was that I would soon be able to do what I wanted without a parent looking over my shoulder.

15

Moving Out?

I soon realised there were a lot of holes in my plan to move out. My mum spent one evening giving me the details of what living on my own entailed: the costs involved and that the best I could hope for was a shared house (I would be living among strangers since I had no friends to share a house with). I was particular about my personal space and the utensils I used. If there was a speck of food on the dishes or cutlery after they had been washed in the dishwasher, I wouldn't use them. As one of my tasks was emptying the dishwasher every morning, I was familiar with bits of food getting stuck to the dishes and I would make a fuss if I had unknowingly put the cutlery in my food.

I was also a germaphobe; I wouldn't sit at the table with my brother at mealtimes if he had a cough or a cold. I didn't want to catch what he had. We were currently in a pandemic, and whilst my family got on my nerves, at least I felt safe that no one was going to bring coronavirus into our house. Mum was the "wash your hands" police!

I think I knew deep down that my family cared about me, but I felt so lost in my head that I couldn't see it. Maybe because I had been discussing moving out and Mum didn't want this to happen. When we extended our home from a three-bedroom to a four-bedroom, I got my own room, but I still had bunkbeds. Mum talked about redecorating, which included getting new furniture and buying me a double bed. I had asked a few times in the past when I would get one.

"When you start keeping your room tidy and stop throwing your clothes on the floor," Mum replied.

I gave it some thought for a minute and then dismissed the idea. It's not that I thought it was a bad idea, but I was fine with how my room was and wouldn't welcome any change.

Around this time, I was doing a lot of research on topics that would have given my parents a heart attack if they had known. I was also seeking advice from online acquaintances whom I felt comfortable with. I had concluded just after the summer of 2020 that there was only one way I could have my independence and be free of my constant loneliness and torment. I wasn't willing to share it with anyone who knew me except the people I knew online.

I had faith in God, but I had given up on praying and talking to God. In the past, Mum had encouraged me to pray and trust God with my problems, and sometimes I felt that my prayers had been answered. But I began questioning: If God was really listening to me, why was I feeling the way I was?

I was curious about what happened after death and tried to discuss this with my brother one day when we were out in the garden doing fitness training.

"What do you think about the afterlife?" I asked him. "Do you think there's life after death? What do you think happens when we die?"

"I don't know," he said. Then, after giving it some thought, he replied, "You should speak to Mum—and anyway, why are you asking?"

"No reason. Just curious."

Around this time there were huge debates going on about George Floyd's murder by the policeman in America, so I used this as an excuse to ask more about the details of what might have happened to him after his death.

I tried not to show too much interest in case my brother got suspicious. I didn't want anyone to know my thoughts and what my plans were. This was one of the reasons I did my research late at night after everyone else had gone to bed.

I could imagine how bad it would be if Mum found out after I'd said nothing was wrong and had refused professional help. I continued to research online, reading academic papers from Oxford and Cambridge on the whos, wheres, and whens on the topics I was interested in. I read about what had been done, and what was successful and what wasn't. In my family I was known for getting things wrong, so I wanted to make sure I got this right. On too many occasions I had rushed into things without giving them proper consideration, and then they backfired on me.

For example, I tried to order a bag for my paper round because the one I had was broken. I ended up ordering three different types of bags, even though Mum had told me to measure the current one and use the size for guidance. I got it wrong three times and had to return two bags. I had to keep the last one because I couldn't return it.

So I had to make sure I got this right. I'd read about those who got it wrong and had to face their family and the aftermath. I couldn't let that happen. I didn't want to live to tell the story afterwards.

I had several conversations with people who I regularly chatted with online. Some were shocked at some of the questions I was asking and encouraged me to speak to my parents or someone professional as I needed help. I was done with that. I had to take matters into my own hands to get the freedom I craved.

My 18th birthday was approaching, and Mum asked me what I wanted. I said I didn't want anything. What was the point? I didn't plan to be here much longer after my 18th birthday, although I had no date in mind. To me it was pointless making my usual list.

To compromise, I told Mum what I wanted to eat. I wasn't going to miss out on one of my favourite food of Chinese tapas. We were subject to very strict lockdown restrictions, so it would only be the four of us, which I was happy about. It had been almost a year of no family gatherings, and in a way I was thankful for that. I'm sure Mum would have wanted to invite family to celebrate my 18th birthday.

16

IS THERE SOMETHING ABOUT DECEMBER?

I had no date or time in mind for when I would do it. I guess when it was the right time, I would know. That was what I told myself.

The night of Thursday, 10th December was like any other night. I had dinner and went up to my room as usual and continued to play Habbo on my laptop. Mum came into my room to tell me to take my laundry downstairs. Soon after she left, I was downstairs with my laundry. She was quite surprised to see me so soon because this wasn't usually the case. I smiled and didn't say anything.

Later I came downstairs and put a pizza in the oven, which I ate later. My brother loaded up the dishwasher and went upstairs to his bedroom. I was alone downstairs, eating the last of my pizza whilst I continued to play Habbo. Before I finished eating, my dad came in to give me some instructions on what I should do in the morning, as I needed to go to the bank and get verified in person so that I could get my Child Trust Fund. I was now 18, and the money would be transferred to my bank account.

As Dad spoke, I thought about the obstacles I had encountered with the form and with getting the money transferred to my account. Something I had thought would be simple had become a problem, with the bank of the Child Trust Fund asking for more information and verification. I thought about Thursday, a week ago, which was my birthday. I'd had my favourite food, and Mum surprised me with lager since I could now legally drink alcohol.

I remember sneakily drinking all four bottles of lager, even though I was only supposed to have one. I thought about the card that Mum and my brother had personally created with pictures of me and special words, and the gifts I had received that I wasn't expecting—two Nike hoodies—even though I had told her I didn't want anything. I thought about the cash gifts from friends and family who had dropped off cards or put money directly into my account. I had received more than one hundred pounds. Then I thought about the disappointment of being forced to buy joggers with some of the money, because Mum said I needed to have something tangible to look back on and not spend it all on McDonald's.

Little did she know I had no plans to be here. I had already taken a big step and ordered a rope the day after my birthday. I knew it was just a matter of time for me to end it.

I heard Dad say, "Did you hear what I said?" and that brought me back to the present and where I was.

"Yes," I responded, looking him in the eye. I wasn't going to tell him I only heard half of what he'd been telling me. In any case I could do it on Monday if I couldn't remember what I needed to do tomorrow. It would annoy him that he would have to repeat it all again, but it didn't matter.

He left me and went upstairs, and I was finally on my own. I finished my pizza, so I went upstairs to my bedroom with no intention of going back downstairs.

Whilst in my bedroom my thoughts went back to my life, as usually happens every night. The call I had with an agency just two days ago came to mind. This was the same agency who had told me when I was looking for a summer job that I was guaranteed a warehouse job when I turned 18. I recalled how excited I was to call him and remind him that I was now 18. The anticipation shrivelled as the same issue cropped up again.

"Are you available for seven days a week? We want someone who is flexible to do any day in the week."

"Errm, I'm looking for part-time work." I had done the same thing as I did at the interview with McDonalds. I could not bear to do full time because of my social anxiety of being around strangers.

I could have kicked myself when he said, "Sorry, we only want someone who can do full-time."

I realised I had messed up again. Mum had told me to say I was available for full time and then afterwards negotiate for part-time hours.

I was frustrated with myself. How was I going to make it if I couldn't hold a simple conversation? I started ruminating over the situations that had gone wrong, all the things I had messed up. I looked up my searches on Google and then I thought, what was stopping me from making tonight the night that I put an end to it?

I had a small bottle of vodka in my room, which I'd bought the day after my birthday since I could now legally buy alcohol. I had the rope; everyone was in bed with no intention of getting up again tonight. Could I do this now? I wondered. What was stopping me?

All I saw in front of me was more of the same. I was already dreading socialising at Christmas (not that there would even be any additional people apart from my immediate family). I knew there was no way I could get out of eating Christmas dinner at the table with my family. My mum had already told me we would all be sitting down at the table for Christmas dinner, as we had done in the past, and this year wouldn't be an exception. We had already had several heated arguments about having Christmas dinner at the dining table. We hadn't sat altogether for months because I'd avoided it since March 2020.

The more I thought about it, the more convinced I was. I had to do it tonight.

I put on one of the hoodies I had got from my parents for my birthday. I got the reel of rope from where I had hidden it and cut a good length with scissors. I practised according to the pictures I had seen on the internet and felt ready.

I carefully went downstairs. I knew my brother usually went to sleep late even though he was already in bed. I was careful not to make any noise going down the stairs. I opened the back door and got the garden chairs I needed for height and leverage.

I got the rope and the vodka. I contemplated doing it in the garage, but I wasn't sure how strong the rods in the roof of the garage were. I put the key to the garage in my pocket because I couldn't be bothered to go back inside the house. I decided to end it by the tree that had a very sturdy branch that could support me.

I hadn't planned it to be this day or night. I hadn't planned it to be this early in the morning of the next day when in a few hours I would have been getting up to do my paper round.

But somehow I knew this was the right time, and I did it.

Part II: The Aftermath of an Irreversible Action

PROLOGUE

There is a pain in my chest, it is a gripping pain almost stopping me from breathing. I have heard of emotional pain feeling like physical pain but never experienced it to this degree. I am feeling suffocated. It's like a ton of weight on my chest that I cannot shift.

I have only experienced something similar once, and this was years ago when we thought we had lost Marley whilst visiting my cousin.

We had gone round by my cousin's house for a birthday celebration. We were all in the living room eating and chatting. Later some of our party moved to the front garden of the house whilst some of us stayed in the living room. I had stayed in the living room when a few minutes later I noticed that Marley was not in the same room as me. I assumed that he was with my auntie in the front garden, but I did not feel right with just assuming, so I got up to check that he was there.

When I got to the front of the house where my cousin and the others were, there was no sign of Marley and they thought he was with me in the living room.

We started searching the house and soon realised he was nowhere in the house, not upstairs or downstairs. My heart was pounding, a fear that I have never experienced was creeping up on me, but I tried not to give in to my horrible imaginations. A toddler cannot disappear in a house. Where could a 2-year-old have gone with four adults in the house? These were some of the questions going through my head.

We started looking for him on the road outside the house and as we crossed the road, we saw him with a group of neighbours who said that they saw him crossing the road by himself and were wondering why he was by himself and trying to ask him who he was. Of course, he was only a toddler and was still learning to speak so they could not make sense of what he was saying. It was such a relief to find him and to hold him.

I could not begin to imagine all the things that could have gone wrong. He could have been run over by a car whilst he was crossing the road by himself, or someone could have snatched him.

I shudder with fear just thinking about it. I was so grateful to God for protecting him and keeping him safe from harm.

That was then and for years after this incidence I made sure that he was always within my sight. For some years afterwards I was very overprotective of him as I did not want to go through those few minutes of not knowing where he was which had felt like hours.

Fast forward sixteen years later and I am here again with this feeling of a ton of weight on my chest, experiencing what I can only imagine feels like several knives being stabbed into my heart. The pain and agony of what I had felt all those years ago when Marley was a toddler could not be compared to what I was feeling now. It was far, far worse than anything I had felt or imagined.

1

Family Life

I was happy. We were a family of four: my husband and two sons. We weren't perfect, but we loved each other, and I made sure that we looked out for each other.

I had a really good career—in fact, I'd say I was almost at the peak of my career. I had never expected, when I came to the UK from Sierra Leone all those years ago, that I would be in an executive position not just looking after the UK and Ireland but also responsible for the rest of Europe.

We had a lovely home with plenty of space, after extending it six years ago, and a spacious garden where we had hosted many barbecues with family and friends.

We didn't have any health issues that weren't under control. I would say we were all in relatively good health; nothing to really cause alarm. I felt we were all in a good place as long as we stayed away from the virus that was taking over the world.

We hadn't long come back from a much-needed holiday in Sierra Leone, the country of my birth. I had reunited with family and friends I hadn't seen for quite a long time.

We had arrived in Sierra Leone on the night of Boxing Day (the day after Christmas), which was on a Thursday, so we could attend my niece's wedding that Saturday. It was a big event, and my husband and sons had never experienced an African wedding. I was really glad they could experience a really traditional celebration—with all the modern elements too, of course.

The traditional music and food on the day before the wedding, known as the bachelor's eve in the Krio culture, the costumes we all had to put on immediately after the church ceremony, the food, and the traditional dancing all contributed to make the holiday very special and gave my family an experience they would remember for years to come.

We also visited one of the natural beaches in the Peninsular and tasted the local cuisine at the houses of different family members and in restaurants. The hot weather of upper twenties and lower thirties centigrade also made the holiday special. Usually at this time of the year in England we would all be wrapped up in winter coats, scarves, and gloves, whilst here in Freetown we were enjoying lovely sunshine, sea, and sand.

The afternoon we left to fly back to England was bittersweet. I said goodbye to family members who were in their late 80s, and I wondered whether this was the last time I would see them on this side of eternity. I gave hugs and kisses with tears in my eyes as I tried to capture the feel and smell of my aunties who had watched me grow up from a baby and now embraced me as a mature woman, wife, and mother of two almost adult children.

And whilst I was concerned that I might not see my aging aunties again, it never crossed my mind that this would be the last time we would go on a holiday as a family of four and that it would be the last time family members in Sierra Leone would see all of us together.

As soon as we got back home, I told my family it was the last time we would all go on holiday together. Well, truer words had never been said! I was thinking about all the stress I'd had trying to get all the necessary vaccinations, visas, and other documentation needed for our travel. Added to this, one family member resisted the pending trip with no valid reason other than what I thought was the social anxiety that he usually experienced when in a crowd.

I had to persevere with every step of the arrangements with Marley telling me he wasn't going. To accommodate him, I booked a hotel, made sure we spent Christmas in England, and only planned the trip to last seven days to ensure that I didn't push him too much out of his comfort zone.

I'm quite sure that anyone would understand why the first thing I said when we were safely back in our house was that I wasn't doing it again!

My sons were fine with my outburst. I expect they were thinking, Who wants to go on holiday with parents when we're aged seventeen and twenty? Definitely young men who wanted to hang out with their own age group and do their own thing. I could tell from their expressions that's what they were thinking.

I slowly got over the stress of the trip and got back into the routine of work and home life. My older son's twenty-first birthday was approaching, and I was having concerns regarding Marley as he had still not agreed to retake his GSCEs. I knew it was already too late for him to take them in May or June because he wasn't prepared.

After putting it off for a while, I had a chat with Marley, and he told me he didn't want to go to college and instead preferred to get a job. In the meantime, he wanted me to give him some time to complete the animation video he had started creating before we went on holiday. I agreed to this, and life went on.

2

CAN WE CELEBRATE, PLEASE?

It was already a month after we arrived back in England and the Covid-19 virus was slowly spreading to different countries, dominating the national news. I wasn't giving it too much attention as I thought that China was very far away, and I had a significant milestone to prepare for. The twenty-first birthday of my elder son was approaching, and I was determined to celebrate the day. I asked him what he wanted to do, and he said, "Nothing, really. Maybe order a takeaway?" which didn't sit well with me—significant birthdays should be celebrated.

"Don't you want me to book dinner for the four of us at a restaurant? It's not every day you get to be twenty-first!"

He agreed to dinner but was reluctant to have a family gathering; he didn't want any fuss. I told him I would keep it small and only invite immediate family. I was excited. I would soon be the mother of a twenty-one-year-old. I started planning; reaching out to immediate family to check availability, planning the menu and digging out photos and videos of infancy. Whilst doing this research I discovered photos and videos of Marley which I had forgotten about.

As the day approached, I realised I was the only one who was excited about the forthcoming celebrations. I didn't realise Marley had no clue about what was happening, because when we' discussed the details, he was in his room and wasn't part of the discussion. He wasn't happy when he found out that he was the last one to know.

I'm glad I pushed through with these plans though. It turned out that this was the last occasion for some of the family to see all of us as a family of four.

The day of his brother's birthday was very difficult; Marley was in a nasty mood. He didn't want to go for dinner and refused to wish his brother a happy birthday. I thought, What's going on now?

I was convinced that this wasn't normal behaviour and made up my mind to get Marley some help the following week, after the birthday celebrations were out of the way. I remember the dinner we had on that Thursday. It was a strange affair. Marley wouldn't interact with us even though he was sitting at the table. He had reluctantly wished his brother Happy Birthday during the journey to the restaurant since I had insisted. His body language spoke volumes; he would rather be anywhere than at dinner with us. He was only there because I wouldn't allow it to be any other way.

The Saturday family gathering was the same. As family members arrived—a total of ten people—he was reluctant to leave his room and greet them. I had to get him downstairs on two occasions to say hello.

Later, he was unhappy and ruminated about feeling awkward when he interacted with family members. I was quite concerned. He had hardly exchanged two words with his cousin, whom he usually got on with very well, during the whole time she was with us. And she had stayed overnight.

The following week I spoke to our private healthcare provider to confirm whether our cover included mental-health care. I was really happy when they said we were covered and thanked God for the company I work at who made this possible. I immediately gave them a summary of what the issues were and asked if someone from the mental-health team could assess him. Assessing him wasn't a problem; getting Marley to cooperate was the challenge!

I wasn't going to give up as I had done before. I knew I could entice him with his favourite food. I told him he had to take the call so he could be assessed as it was very obvious to me that something wasn't right. It was not normal that all he wanted to do was sleep and surfaced only to eat or do his paper round.

He took the call and was later diagnosed with mild depression. He was prescribed ten sessions with a therapist but only attended one. He kept telling me nothing was wrong with him, and he didn't need therapy.

As a mother you are torn between pushing or holding off. Were these just symptoms of normal teenage hormonal behaviour that he would grow out of, or was this something more? These are the sort of questions I was battling.

He had only attended the first therapy session before the UK was locked down because of coronavirus. Later, I found out from the therapist that he didn't disclose anything that would have indicated his suicidal thoughts. He had mentioned his social anxiety but nothing more, so there was no way he could have been diagnosed with something more serious than just mild depression. Since we were in lockdown after the first session, he couldn't continue with the therapy. It was put on hold until he could physically meet with the therapist again.

I had to think of ways to keep him out of his room. I came up with another solution to get him out of his room. He loved pizza and junk food, so I promised him more of these in the weekly shopping if he would do daily training sessions with his brother in the garden. For me it was more about getting him outside away from his numerous screens—TV, tablet, laptop, and mobile phone—and getting some exercise as I had read somewhere that this was good for depression.

This solution was fraught with arguments and disagreements between the two brothers. Since the only exercise Marley did was ride his bike for his paper round, he found it difficult to keep up with the training sessions his brother had put together for him. I had to intervene quite often because Marley was complaining it was too hard and he couldn't do it, but he still wanted the extra treats I had promised him. I asked his brother to go easy on him, make it lighter to start off with until he got used to it.

All through the summer they persevered until it got to the point where his brother's patience ran out.

I decided to try something different. Since he was still refusing to continue with the therapy sessions, even though some of the lockdown restrictions had been lifted, I told Marley to do his own exercise, as long as he recorded it and shared it in our WhatsApp family chat group. Then he would get the additional pizzas and junk food he wanted.

He seemed happy with this, and I thought at least he would continue to release endorphins, which I understood triggered a positive feeling in the body. I thought this would be good for him and would improve how he felt about himself, which, in turn, might help shift the mild depression he had been diagnosed with.

I had no clue there were deeper and more alarming issues than those that had been diagnosed.

3

Never Saw This Coming

We were now into autumn, and I was seeing a difference in Marley. He wasn't as defensive and was more receptive to being corrected. I was pleasantly surprised when one evening he agreed to watch a movie downstairs with his brother. I remember being in bed and saying to his dad, "What a change in Marley." I never thought I would see the day when he would sit in the front room and watch a movie with his brother as he had become such a hermit, always in his room.

I was really pleased, and the next day I asked his brother, "How was your movie night with Marley?"

He responded that it had been a bit weird as Marley wouldn't stop talking. He had talked so much that afterwards he said his jaw was hurting. I found it strange that he had talked right through the movie but thought that maybe he was making up for all the time he hadn't interacted with us.

I continued to see small changes in him, and I was happy that he wasn't always running off to his room after mealtimes. I really thought things were changing for the better. I assumed the daily exercise was having an impact on his well-being.

I asked him what he wanted for his 18th birthday, which was a few weeks away. I wanted to be prepared. There was no plan to book a table for dinner because of coronavirus, so whatever we did would have to involve only the four of us and take place at home.

He declined any presents, even though I thought he would have jumped at the chance to get a new bike or something he needed. He conceded a little by telling me what he would like for dinner on his birthday. As with his brother, I refused to accept that he wanted nothing for his birthday and decided to get him something he had asked for during the summer. When I had got him some T-shirts in the summer, he also asked for Nike hoodies, so I ordered him two nice ones. I created a personalised birthday card for him online.

I was late ordering the birthday items and wasn't sure they would arrive in time. Fortunately, the hoodies and the card arrived on the day of his birthday, so we were able to give him the gifts and card. He wasn't overjoyed—that was his usual demeanour over the last two years—but at least he said thank you. I was a bit disappointed. I thought he would have been impressed with the personalised card. Later I found out that he'd told his brother he really liked it, even though he hadn't told me. Though we could not have family over, I made a video call to his auntie so she could see him and wish him happy birthday. There were also lots of calls from family and friends far and near.

With everything that had been going on, you would expect that I would have seen what was coming, but I didn't. None of us did. We were completely blindsided with no warning.

I shared with Marley that he would be getting his Child Trust Fund, which the government had started when he was born, and now that he was 18, the money would be transferred to his bank account. It would be his to spend however he wanted. I really thought he would be excited, but he seemed to just take in his stride with no outward emotion.

On a cold, cloudless December morning, I experienced the most traumatic event of my life.

I woke up quite early, as usual, to have a quiet time of prayer and reading my Bible and a devotional. I read the verse of the day and then went on to read about a woman named Martha who was in a refugee camp and had experienced the traumatic loss of her family; rebels had broken into her home and killed her husband and two of her sons whilst she and her 6-month-old son hid. I couldn't begin to imagine the pain and agony she must have gone through and silently asked, "God, how could you have allowed this to happen?"

Little did I know that Martha's story was preparing me for what I would be facing in a little under two hours. I was also astounded by Martha's faith and joy, which the author of the devotional wanted to bring to light. Despite the tragic loss of her family, she was full of joy, supporting the other refugees in the camp and ministering to them.

I finished my quiet time and proceeded to get ready for work. It was a Friday, the end of my work week. I was looking forward to some downtime, but of course I had to get through Friday first.

As I prepared for working from home, I went downstairs to boot up my laptop, turn off the outside light, and open the curtains. I was surprised that the light was still on, as this indicated that Marley hadn't left for his paper round. I checked the back door as is my usual routine but didn't realise the door wasn't locked until I came back downstairs the second time. I took out the washing from the washing machine with the intention of taking the bedsheets to hang outside when I came back downstairs.

Second time round, I noticed the back door leading to the garden wasn't locked with the key and assumed my younger son had left it unlocked after leaving for his paper round early in the morning. I thought he had got up when I went back upstairs.

I went back upstairs again and finished off getting ready whilst informing my husband that the back door was unlocked and our youngest must have left it open in his rush not to be late for his paper round.

I was back downstairs for the third time, and since it was cloudy and cold, I thought I would only hang out the bedsheet and put the rest of the clothing on the clothes airer.

I grabbed the navy-blue sheet, opened the door leading to the garden from the utility room, and saw something that no mother ever wants to see. Am I awake? I asked myself. Am I really seeing what I'm seeing? Is it my imagination or is the sight in front of me for real? I must be in a trance because this can't be real. It's not true; it must be a mirage.

In those few seconds, which felt like hours, I refused to accept that what I was seeing was reality. I felt I must still be asleep and having a nightmare.

I was in shock. I couldn't move for those few seconds, and then I shouted, "Marley, Marley!"

The sound of my voice didn't even seem like mine. I ran towards the mirage that unfortunately was reality.

From afar I had wondered who was standing under the tree in the garden. The person looked like Marley but appeared to be too tall. The clothes and trainers were Marley's, but with his back facing me, I couldn't tell whether it was really him. My head was also telling me that Marley had gone to do his paper round, so I couldn't work out why he would be standing under the tree.

God in his faithfulness knew I couldn't take the magnitude of the traumatic incident unfolding in front of me in one go, so it came to me in bits. When I got closer, I realised Marley was hanging with a rope round his neck tied to the tree. My immediate reaction was to try to get him off the tree, but I couldn't, so I had to rush into the house screaming for his dad and his brother as they were still in bed.

They rushed downstairs. They couldn't make sense of what I was saying, because I was crying and talking at the same time. I was shaking, but I managed to give them instructions to get him off the tree and bring him into the house. I really thought he had just passed out and could be revived. I was praying to God for miracles, I couldn't believe my baby boy was gone. In between the crying, I had managed to call the emergency services and the paramedics were on their way.

Meanwhile, before the paramedics arrived, I felt that I had to pray to God to bring him back. He's only eighteen, I thought, and only last week we celebrated his birthday and told him what he could do now that he was legally considered an adult.

I threw myself on him as his dad and brother laid him on the floor of the utility room.

"Jesus," I prayed, "you are the healer. You brought Lazarus back from the dead after three days, I'm trusting you now to bring Marley back. How could you take him? He has all his life ahead of him."

The paramedics arrived and asked us to go into the other room. They closed the door, and the three of us looked at each other in disbelief and despair. His brother was in tears, pacing the floor. I was crying and asking God why? I wasn't sure whether I was awake or still sleeping, and my husband was trying to be strong for all three of us.

It felt like an hour, but it was only ten minutes or so before one of the paramedics opened the door and told us that unfortunately, Marley was gone, and there was nothing more they could do.

I heard this wailing and didn't even recognise it was me until his brother put his arms around me to comfort me. I was devastated. I kept thinking I must still be asleep as it wasn't even half past nine yet. This couldn't be real.

4

BREAKING THE NEWS

It was the evening of that traumatic day. The minutes and hours had flown by without me realising that the day was almost gone. I had made calls to family members and close friends shortly after we had the confirmation of death. The calls were really difficult to make. No one expected such devastating news.

The police later flooded the house to rule out any suspicious activity. They did forensics in his room, asked us questions, and took pictures of the tree and the immediate surroundings. We had discovered that he had the key to the garage in his pocket. A small, empty vodka bottle lay on the grass underneath the tree. The garden chairs were stacked together, with one chair directly underneath where I had found him hanging.

I had lots of questions without answers.

Slowly, we started piecing things together. The police had unlocked his phone, and in his Google searches, we saw that he had been researching ways to end his life. In his notepad he had also reflected on what would happen when someone ends his life and no longer had a physical body to do the things they used to do. We were shocked and unable to believe that our Marley, the youngest in the family, who wasn't streetwise and always needed a guiding hand, could have orchestrated this fatal act right underneath our noses without us having the slightest inkling of what he was planning.

In the midst of my despair, I recalled the devotional I had read in my quiet time that morning, the story about Martha, who had witnessed the murder of her husband and two sons whilst hiding from the rebels who had invaded her home. I really felt comforted. God has a way of speaking to us and preparing us for things to come. The story of Martha was God's way of preparing me for what I would go through when I discovered what Marley had done.

By now it was late in the evening, and I realised none of us had eaten or drunk anything all day apart from a few hot drinks.

Close family had come round and had now gone, and I had to find the strength to prepare some food for us. Nothing heavy, as we weren't hungry, but I knew we had to eat to keep our strength.

After we went through the motions of eating, there were still close family members who weren't aware of what had happened. I was conscious of how I shared this very sad and unexpected news. I called his godmother and asked her where she was as I didn't want to share the news if she was driving or in a public place. She knew everything about Marley; we had spent the last eighteen years praying and fasting for our children every first Saturday of the month.

She told me she was in the laundrette, so I asked her to call me when she was home, which turned out to be about an hour later. I knew how blindsided we were by discovering Marley this morning and tried to prepare everyone before I told them the horrible news. How do you share such devastating news with anyone who knew Marley as a quiet young man in good physical health with no noticeable illness?

It was hard. Everyone I told fell apart on the phone, totally devastated. In some cases, I was the one offering words of comfort. In other cases, it caused me to grieve all over again.

In the midst of my despair, there was also some anger. "How could Marley have thrown us into the spotlight when he hated the spotlight himself?" I asked myself.

I recalled questions upon questions from the police and the number of police cars outside the house. So many vehicles, in fact, that one of our neighbours had been texting me asking why. We had lived in this house for nearly seventeen years, and not once had we been the centre of attention. In their investigations, the police had to interview our immediate neighbours to ask if they had observed anything suspicious in the hours leading up to Marley's death.

Whilst I tried to prepare family and friends when I spoke to them before breaking the news about Marley, there were a few with whom I had been very blunt and direct in my narrative. One of these was my line manager. I was supposed to have joined an online meeting with her and another colleague, a regular meeting that we had every Friday. She had texted me and I was trying to text her back when she called me. I immediately started crying and just blurted out everything that had happened prior to her call.

At the time the house was still full of police, and I told her in gruesome detail what had happened and how I had found Marley. Later on, I would reflect back on that conversation and apologise to her for being so blunt, but at the same time I had to commend her for the way she handled such a critical moment. I will always remember her encouraging words in the midst of tears as she couldn't stop herself from being emotional after hearing such devastating news.

Another conversation during which I was brutally blunt was the call with the newsagent who employed Marley to do the paper round. We had seen a text message he had sent Marley when he hadn't turned up for his paper round that Friday morning. It wasn't a very encouraging message and it made me mad. I started thinking of all the times Marley had said he had been told he would lose his paper round if he was late again, and I knew how devastating that would have been for him.

Marley's phone was still unlocked and suddenly started ringing. It was a call from the newsagent. His brother didn't know whether he should answer so I took the phone from him and answered it.

The newsagent's first words were, "Where are you?"

As soon as I heard him, expecting to speak to Marley, asking where he was and not checking to see if he was OK, I just saw red and gave it to him straight. "Marley has killed himself."

He was stunned. I knew I had handled it badly, but I was high on emotion and wanted to lash out at someone, and he was the ideal candidate. At a later date, when he came round to properly sympathise, I shared some truths with him. I said that I considered him to be a kind of mentor to these young ones, as their first experience of earning money could be as a paperboy or papergirl. At that age they have no idea of the rules of earning a living. I told him he had an opportunity to mentor and coach and not be the hard taskmaster Marley had painted him to be in some instances.

Whether he took on board what I said I don't know, but I was glad I said my piece. I hope he did listen, for the sake of all the other young ones like Marley who depended on the paper round for that little bit of independence.

5

SURROUNDED BY LOVE

I thought that the emotional roller coaster of the first day would be over in the coming days. I wasn't prepared for the firsts. The first time I came downstairs the next morning was tough. The night before, we had hardly slept. I lay in bed thinking about what had happened, swaying between a sort of reality and a dreamlike state, not sure if someone was going to wake me up and tell me it was a nightmare, that it didn't really happen, whilst all the images kept going round and round in my head. I couldn't get rid of them no matter how hard I tried. I would later realise it is hard to get rid of these images.

I couldn't stay in bed any longer after tossing and turning all night. I got up and went downstairs. It was about five thirty in the morning and I could hear Marley's alarm for his paper round going off on his phone, even though the phone was off. I went to his room and took the phone downstairs with me. Seeing that the outside light was still on got me emotional as Marley was always the first downstairs and he would turn off the light.

I started crying and praying at the same time. I was crying to God, asking where Marley was now. After bringing him up in church and taking him to Sunday school, I wanted assurance that he was with Jesus. I recalled all the conversations we'd about God and the prayers we had shared. I recalled him telling me once that it was like he had two voices speaking to him sometimes, and he knew it was the devil and Jesus, but he didn't listen to the devil.

I was down on my knees on the floor of the utility room where the day before I had been crying to God to raise him back to life. Now I was asking God to let me know that he had him. If Marley wasn't here with me, where I could continue to nurture him, I needed the assurance that he was in heaven.

Whilst I was praying silently and sobbing loudly, his brother came downstairs and gave me a hug. He said, "Marley is at peace. He is no longer troubled."

I immediately felt a calmness and assurance that I couldn't explain. I felt the peace according to what is written in the Bible:

> "And the peace of God [that peace which reassures the heart, that peace] which transcends all understanding, [that peace which] stands guard over your hearts and minds in Christ Jesus [is yours]"
>
> (Philippians 4:7 Amplified Bible)

Another first was unloading the dishwasher. I started and couldn't finish, as it was a stark reminder that Marley would never do this again. This was Marley's chore that he did every morning after his paper round. Even when he was still at school, he unloaded the dishwasher before going to school. On this occasion, his brother had to finish.

The cupboard and freezer were full of the food he loved, as our monthly shopping had only been delivered two days before his demise. Looking at all the food that only Marley loved, I burst into tears. I experienced what almost felt like physical stabs to my heart. I was sobbing and devastated all over again.

I turned to God. "How could you let this happen?" I asked in my despair. Never to see that cheeky smile again. Never to hear him talk to me and exchange opinions. It was hard; it was unbearable, but I had to hold on, and I could only do it with the help of God.

I have lost close family members: my dad, my mum, siblings, aunties, and cousins, but nothing prepared me for the pain and emptiness of losing a child. It definitely wasn't the normal order of how things should be. As parents, we're supposed to die before our children, not the other way round.

In the midst of my despair, I heard a voice say to me, "I would not let you be tempted more than you can handle. Of all the alternatives available, this was the one that you could bear, which is why I allowed it."

I started to think about what some of these alternatives could have been. Marley could have been unsuccessful in taking his life, but in the process he could have damaged his brain and never been the same again. Or we could have got there just after he lost consciousness and saved him, but then forever lived in fear of him doing it again as all trust would have been eroded.

This verse came to mind:

> No temptation [regardless of its source] has overtaken or enticed you that is not common to human experience [nor is any temptation unusual or beyond human resistance]; but God is faithful [to His word—He is compassionate and trustworthy], and He will not let you be tempted beyond your ability [to resist], but along with the temptation He [has in the past and is now and] will [always] provide the way out as well, so that you will be able to endure it [without yielding and will overcome temptation with joy].
>
> (1 Corinthians 10:13 AMP)

The first time going into his room was tough. It was a mess, what with the untidy state Marley kept it in, plus all the debris the police had left after their investigation. A few days later I felt the urge to tidy it up. I pushed through the pain as I realised it needed to be done. His room wasn't going to be that part of the house we didn't dare visit. I tidied up a bit and threw away all the rubbish.

The next day after he was gone, was the first Saturday when we did the deep cleaning as a family, this was really difficult. None of us felt like it; it would be too hard. Who would clean the mirrors and do the dusting, not to mention the vacuuming, which was Marley's task? None of us fancied it. So, we did a little tidying and left it for another day.

We constantly got phone calls as the news spread from one family member or friend to the other. I couldn't tell everyone, so there were some family members given the task of telling others and, likewise, the same for friends. We spent that weekend trying to tell all our close friends and family members. Cards and flowers were being delivered in a steady stream from people far and wide.

The love we received was overwhelming, and we were thankful to know that people cared for us. But at the same time we were having to repeat some of the same answers over and over again to the same questions, as most people asked the same things: "Were there any signs?" "Did you know he was suicidal?" We found this quite overwhelming.

One of my friends asked me what I wanted from her and how she could support me. At the time I had no clue what I wanted or needed. I had never lost a child before. I didn't know what to say to her. She immediately said she would bring food the next day and later organised a rota for all the local friends who wanted to bring food. We didn't want two or three people delivering food on the same day.

In the months that followed she also organised a few friends to deliver something on the eleventh of each month to cheer me up. Sometimes it was flowers, sometimes a fruit basket, and sometimes something to pamper myself. Another close friend also decided she would bake a cake every two weeks and drop it off.

Our pastor was also very supportive. He turned up with a bagful of goodies, from facial tissues to a box of chocolates; cleaning stuff for the dishwasher, mousse for hair—it seemed everything was in that bag. He helped us get the gate fixed as well because, in the rush for the emergency services to get into our house on the day, the gate had been kicked down and was hanging by a nail. He was also supportive when we needed to go to the funeral home and make the arrangements.

These and many more tokens of love kept us going during the first few weeks. I remember another friend deciding to cook and serve soup in takeaway cups for us to have at the cemetery, since it was a cold day, and we couldn't have a repast because of the Covid restrictions.

Friends prayed with me every single day, and others prayed with me fortnightly, and of course I continued with my monthly fast and prayer. Other friends went for walks with me so that I got out of the house and had some fresh air. At the time it wasn't obvious to me how much I needed this until I got outside. I realised that only God could see me through this. If he wasn't going to stop it, then he already had a plan for me to get through it.

I was constantly playing or singing this song about God's goodness (written by Jason Ingram, Ed Cash, Brian Mark Johnson, Jenn Louise Johnson, and Ben David Fielding):

From "Goodness of God"
I love You, Lord. . . .
I love Your voice.

You have led me through the fire
In the darkest night.
You are close like no other.
I've known You as a Father.
I've known You as a Friend,
And I have lived in the goodness of God (yeah)

This song was my daily anthem. I needed to remind myself that all my life, God has been faithful; he hadn't suddenly abandoned me because I lost Marley. He is still the same God. He still loves me the same. I was also touched when I received a letter from a resident of one of the houses Marley delivered newspapers to during his paper round. This elderly man, who had the same name as my husband, had taken the time to share with us how Marley had helped him set up payments for his newspapers at the height of the lockdown, as he was shielding and couldn't go out to pay for them. Marley had never mentioned it, and I felt comforted that he was being helpful to others as we had taught him from a young age.

6

STAYING STRONG

The pain didn't decrease; the pain in my heart didn't lessen. I was constantly swaying from one emotion to another: Guilt for not realising Marley was going through much deeper mental anguish than I had thought, anger that he should have taken such an action without sharing his feelings with us, sadness because I felt he had taken a lonely journey while we were all asleep in bed, fear of losing anyone else in our family, and helpless because there was nothing I could do to bring him back.

Surprisingly, I felt I was drawing closer to God, for, as the Bible says,

> "The Lord is near to the heartbroken and He saves those who are crushed in spirit (contrite in heart, truly sorry for their sin)."
>
> (Psalm 34:18 AMP)

Marley's photos and videos, the ones we had taken over the years, and especially when he was younger, were a source of comfort to me.

My husband asked me, "Why are you watching that? Doesn't it make you sad?"

I had said no, because if anything, it brought him back to life. We had captured a memory of a moment in time when he was laughing or talking or doing everyday stuff. When I yearned to hear his voice, I listened to some of the last WhatsApp voice messages he had sent me telling me something or asking me to get something from the supermarket on my way home.

I discovered in those early days that though we all loved Marley in our family, the relationship we shared with him was very different. The mother-son relationship was very strong, having carried him for more than nine months in the womb, I had always been his go-to person when he needed anything. It was usually the two of us in the morning trying to step out of each other's way as we prepared our breakfast when he got home from his paper round.

There was emptiness when I got downstairs first thing, and for weeks after his death I would be in tears, missing our special moments.

It was only the Monday of that same week that he had come back from his paper round with issues with his bike.

"I should have asked for a new bike when you asked me what I wanted for my birthday," he had said.

"Really, it's not too late. I could still get you a new bike."

"Nah."

Even though I had bought him Christmas gifts already, I would have got him the bike too as I usually liked to get gifts that are needed. Instead, he told his dad about his latest bike issues, as he usually fixed any issues that didn't need a bike specialist.

When I think of that week, a few things caused me to ponder. Marley asked me for things I would normally have refused because he already had them, but for some reason it was as if my spirit knew this was my last opportunity to say yes and that I would regret it later if I said no.

For example, he loved apple pies and already had a box of six from the shopping, which was delivered on the Tuesday before his death on the Friday. On the Wednesday, he asked if he could have some from the other box of six, and usually I would have said no and told him that there were other people in the house who hadn't yet had their share, but on this occasion I said yes. He also asked for some Pringles, which I gave him, and the remainder of the pack was later found in his room. He went on to ask me for my can of Coke, which I would generally have refused him, and for once I actually said yes. He was quite surprised at the time!

These were little things that I recalled later on, and it gave me peace that I had said yes when usually I would have said no.

As we huddled together in our grief on that fateful day, one of the first things we had to do was get the tree cut down. I made a call on the very day he passed to get the tree taken away, as it was one of the first things that we found difficult: going into the garden and seeing the tree brought it all back.

Two days later the tree was gone, and we could breathe a bit more freely. I sometimes wonder why he had the key to the garage in his pocket. He had no reason to have gone into the garage as he hadn't hidden the rope there. We later found the whole reel of rope in his room behind his chest of drawers. I concluded that he must have thought of doing it in the garage, but the rods holding the roof may not have looked strong enough. Since he wanted to ensure it was a successful action, he didn't want to take a chance.

I really thank God that it wasn't in the house or the garage as we would have found it difficult to stay here. As it is, because it was outside and on a tree, we could easily get rid of the tree whilst creating a flowerbox where the tree had been as a memory to Marley.

The Bible says, "In every situation [no matter what the circumstances] be thankful and continually give thanks to God; for this is the will of God for you in Christ Jesus" (1 Thessalonians 5:18 AMP).

There are several interpretations to this verse, but I always look at it this way: we should always be thankful because we're created to be grateful. It's God's will for us to be thankful. Whatever the situation, there is usually a worse position that you could be in than whatever your circumstances are.

Some may disagree with me, but I can't imagine the emotions of other mums like Martha (in my devotional) or countless other women who have lost their sons due to someone taking their lives. For me, though, that wasn't how it happened, and Marley wasn't killed by someone else. Though he wasn't in a good mental state when he made the decision to end his life, no one took his life away from him.

7

Difficult Days

How we got through the pain of Christmas Day without Marley, God only knows. We tried doing something different from what we would normally do and ate Christmas dinner in front of the television instead of at the dinner table. There was no way we could handle sitting at the dining table as it would have been unbearable to have three place settings instead of the usual four, with one significant person missing at the table. It was bearable doing something different.

I gave Marley's Christmas gifts to friends of his who would appreciate them, as I didn't want to see them in the house after the person they were intended for was no longer with us.

After Christmas Day we had to prepare for the viewing at the funeral home and then the service itself. I was so thankful that we could have the burial before the New Year. We had agreed with our pastor and the funeral home that we would have the service on Tuesday, 29 December 2020.

Planning the service, putting together the order of service, and working out who, out of the numerous family members and friends, would attend in person, along with those who had played a part in Marley's young life and who wanted to have the opportunity to do something in the service, was a challenge. We made it work, especially writing the eulogy. It was definitely a family affair put together by the three of us and his cousin, who read the eulogy.

As a family we grew stronger, because, with strict lockdown at the time, we couldn't have anyone from outside our household visiting. All food deliveries had to be made at the door. We had to be dependent on each other with regular check-ins on how we were feeling. As an individual I grew stronger as I learned to lean more on God than anyone else.

I still had lots of questions and over the course of time I started getting answers. Some of those answers came from unexpected sources. I spoke to a close confidante on Christmas Day, and she told me about a friend who was moving to another country because her son had tried to take his life and was now sectioned, so she couldn't bear to stay in England anymore. I reflected on that, and I realised that I would have found it really hard to bear if Marley had ended up in a similar situation.

When I kept thinking about why he had done it and where his head was at the time, I had a dream in which Marley said to me "I'm sorry, I'm sorry, I was having dark, dark thoughts." I felt comforted because in the dream his voice was so clear to me, and it was almost as if I was awake.

In early January about a month after his demise, I discovered that he had been researching this for a long time and conversing with different people online. I also found out what day he had ordered the rope and why we had no inkling as usually either my husband or I will be the ones to receive any delivery. He had the foresight to get it delivered to a collection point and not to our house. He was determined not to be found out. I imagined the fallout if we had found out before he did it. How would he have felt and how would we have felt? I concluded that it would have been terrible, as all trust would have been gone.

A week after Marley passed, I got the strong impression that I needed to do something with my pain. A few people had asked how I wanted to remember Marley, and I couldn't think clearly then. But later it became clear to me from this scripture, which was one of the readings at the service for Marley.

The Bible says, "I assure you and most solemnly say to you, unless a grain of wheat falls into the earth and dies, it remains alone [just one grain, never more]. But if it dies it produces much more grain and yields a harvest" (John 12:24 AMP).

I felt this compelling need to help other children who are experiencing the same or similar mental illness as Marley.

If this traumatic incident hadn't happened, I would never have thought of that. Since it had, I had an opportunity to turn my pain into something beneficial for others. The idea to combine what Marley loved to do and the struggle he had with anxiety and depression gave birth to Marley's Aart Foundation (https://www.marleysaartfoundation.com/). Somehow, I had to use art to help those with similar mental health issues.

Soon after, I got confirmation from a close family friend whilst she was praying with me. Her daughter had a dream, and in the dream Marley was all dressed up, looking relaxed, teaching, and supporting children with art.

I shared with her the inspiration I'd recently had, and we both said this was confirmation.

8

Hope Amid Pain

The day of Marley's burial was very difficult, but surprisingly it got better as the day unfolded. The night before the service—and I say service because I still can't say the word funeral—I remember thinking, How will I get through tomorrow?

I knew the itinerary by heart—what time the hearse would leave the funeral home, what time it would arrive at our house, and the route it would take to the church. I had given the funeral home the route as this was the way we had gone so many times before. I was wondering if I would be able to compose myself; waves of uncontrollable loss rolled over me from moment to moment.

> The Bible says, "'Listen to Me,' [says the Lord], 'O house of Jacob, and all the remnant of the house of Israel, You who have been carried by me from your birth and have been carried [in my arms] from the womb, even to your old age I am He, and even to your advanced old age I will carry you!

I have made you and I will carry you; be assured I will carry, and I will save you.'"

(Isaiah 46:3–4 AMP)

These verses really spoke to me and reminded me that God was with me and would continue to be with me.

When I needed something to hold on to, God in his amazing love reminded me about something I had experienced earlier in 2020 when I was travelling back to England on my way home from a business trip. I had looked out the window of the plane and saw a plane in the clouds surrounded by what looked like a rainbow or a ring of fire, travelling parallel to us. After a few seconds of watching this image in awe and wonder, I took my phone and recorded it. I wanted to capture this amazing image.

As I continued to watch, it dawned on me that the plane I could see was the plane I was on—the sun had projected the image that I was seeing on the clouds. I was amazed at the awesomeness of God. The ring of rainbow or fire was telling me that God is in control, that he was the one carrying us in this plane.

I have travelled a lot for business and for pleasure, but the incredible achievement of a plane being in the air never gets old for me. Whilst there is a lot I do not understand about the physics of it all, there is one thing I know for sure: God gave human beings the brains and know-how to do and create such amazing things. I didn't know how much this would come to mean to me later in the year, but at that time I felt this assurance that

God's got me, and he wanted to show me in a physical way by allowing me to see this through the window.

As I reflected on this, I felt that the same God would be with me through the difficult day in front of me and the days ahead. I thought about how it feels for a parent to bury a child, as it is not the normal order of how things should be. And I thought about burying my own son, for whom I had so many hopes and dreams and ambitions, and I broke down in tears.

The hours leading up to the arrival of the hearse at our house were torture. I had felt the emotions bubbling underneath the surface, and my hands shook as I put on my white dress. We had agreed that the colour for all the women attending the service would be white, representing innocence.

It was an effort to get ready. I kept looking out the window, thinking about the number of times in the past when I would get ready for work and look out this very window. I would see Marley's friend, who later moved north, waiting for him so they could ride to school together. Later on, after he left school, I looked out the window and saw him coming home from his paper round. And now I couldn't believe I would never see him on his bike again.

When I heard the doorbell ring, I knew the hearse was outside. I couldn't stop myself from breaking down into uncontrollable tears. I heard the funeral director speaking to me and the words, "Sorry for your loss," but the rest of it was just noise in the background as I looked at the hearse and tried to comprehend that Marley, my Marley, was in that vehicle.

Because of strict lockdown restrictions we couldn't have a car for the family, but my friend had volunteered to be our chauffeur for the day, and somehow she managed to lead me to her car. We all got in and were on our way. I was sitting in the back with Marley's brother, and through my tears I saw some of my neighbours outside and along the road adjacent to our house. I also saw a couple from our church who lived quite close to us standing by the roadside paying their respects.

I was crying uncontrollably, and even the song that was my anthem ("Goodness of God," sung by Tasha Cobbs Leonard) couldn't stop the tears from flowing down my face.

When we got to the church, some of my friends from the Ladies Bible Study group stood opposite the church as we walked in. I was really touched, and this really comforted me. Indeed, God was carrying me through this. Though I couldn't physically see him, the love and commitment from the ladies, standing outside for the seventy-five-minute service because they couldn't go inside due to Covid restrictions, said a thousand words. I was grateful, and as the service commenced, I got stronger and focused on celebrating Marley's shorter-than-expected life.

After the burial we lingered for a while at the cemetery, a time of reflection and refreshments for those who had attended the funeral, since there couldn't be a repast or reception indoors. Through the foresight of a friend, we had soup served in takeaway cups to keep us warm. I had some time to show gratitude to all who had attended, including a few family members and friends who had travelled from Oxford, London, Reading,

Kent, and Northampton, all of us united in our grief, each trying to make sense of it all.

Later when we arrived home, there were mixed emotions. On one hand this terrible day was almost over, but with it was also the finality of burial. Our close friends from Reading had followed us home as I had brought over some gifts from friends in Sierra Leone earlier in the year that they needed to collect. In a way it was good that we had this diversion because if we hadn't, we would have been on our own soon after we were dropped off. Whilst they couldn't enter the house, we chatted with them outside and felt comforted by their presence.

Later I spoke to my brother in Sierra Leone and was touched when he told me that even in the pandemic, about fifty people consisting of family and close friends had attended the service they had at their house directly after streaming the service for Marley on YouTube. I was told it was emotional and there were tears over there as cousins and aunties also paid tribute to Marley. On YouTube, I later saw all the messages that had been left by friends and family from all over the world.

Again, as before, I was touched how God had used so many people to show me love and comfort during a difficult period. With the time difference in America, I was amazed that even friends and family from that side of the ocean had joined the live service.

9

Being Comforted

As a family, we're still navigating the aftermath of losing Marley, but we're moving forward with Marley in our hearts. There are difficult days ahead, such as the opening of the inquest and the actual inquest hearing. I had already spoken several times to the coroner's officer. A death such as suicide would always be reported to the coroner. The coroner's officer, on behalf of the coroner, will try to gain a better understanding of what happened to the person who took his own life. They gather evidence and information to help understand the circumstances leading to that suicide. They are required to start the process as soon as possible, and this is known as opening an inquest. This is usually a brief meeting in the coroner's court, allowing them to adjourn (postpone) the full inquest to a later date to allow sufficient time for information to be gathered. I hope I will be feeling stronger when we have to attend the inquest.

The Bible says, "When you pass through the waters, I will be with you; and through the rivers, they will not overwhelm you. When you walk through the fire, you will not be scorched, nor will the flame burn you" (Isaiah 43:2 AMP).

God promises to be with us in all these different situations. We feel the waters as we go through the river, feel the splashing of the water, feel the force of it trying to pull us under—just as the traumatic event of Marley's suicide tried to pull us down into grief—but we weren't in any way submerged by it because every step of the way, God was letting us know he was there. The image of what we saw in the garden on that fateful day was imprinted in our memories and may be for a very long time. In those early days we couldn't shake it from our thoughts, and from moment to moment we felt the heat of it, but we weren't burned even though there were times when it felt like it.

God cares, and we're reminded of this on a daily basis. Our pastor reminded us in his message on the day of the service; we don't have the answers to all the questions we have regarding Marley's death, but God still cares.

The support of our church family and our friends and relations has been tremendous. The individual professional counselling we had in the first ten weeks after the burial helped us open up and talk about Marley. We're constantly reminiscing about what he would think or do in different situations we have experienced without him.

For instance, when it was his brother's 22nd birthday, we decided we would have a McDonald's meal in honour of Marley. I ordered a Big Mac for myself as this was Marley's favourite.

When I introduced a new meal into our dinnertime, I said to his brother, "Guess who would have loved this meal?"

He immediately said Marley because it included a burger and fries.

When I received a Google Nest home automation system as a Christmas gift from work, we all immediately said that Marley would have taken great pleasure in saying, "Hey, Google, can you tell me this or that?" He was very opinionated and always liked to have the last word and would have loved to prove he was right by asking Google Nest. We're constantly bringing his name into our conversations to keep his memory alive.

When his brother tripped in the garden because it was slippery, he couldn't help but think that Marley would have laughed his head off if he could have seen him, and maybe he did see him because he was there in spirit. Only God knows.

When I reached out for a tissue from the box and realised there were none because someone had taken the last one, I had to say, "Sorry, Marley. I thought you were the only one who left the tissue box empty after taking the last one, but now I know it wasn't only you."

Whilst we move forward and take him with us, we know that family celebrations and events will never be the same, and for me, the eleventh as a date will always bring back memories of Marley. When the date and the day of the week coincide, it will always be harder but knowing that there is a legacy that will help others will continue to give me hope and spur me on.

Amongst all the love and support we were shown daily, I was pleasantly surprised when my manager from my previous employers told me she had written a song about Marley. She felt inspired after watching the service on YouTube for a second time and felt that the words of the song were given to her. God indeed works and moves in mysterious ways.

10

Be Encouraged

I'm a Christian and have a very strong faith in God. Not everyone will understand the Bible references in the latter chapters, but I included the references and the gospel song for those who will understand the context and draw strength from them. I'm aware that there will be a lot of people from other faiths or religions who will read this book, and I would like to say I can only refer to what I know and what has really been my source of strength during this difficult time. There are also others who have no faith or religion, and I hope you are also able to get something out of reading this book.

I would like to encourage any parent who has children who are showing similar symptoms to Marley's to follow your gut feeling. Sometimes as parents we can only do what we can with the knowledge we have, so don't beat yourself up if you don't always get it right. Being a parent is something none of us received formal training for. In some cases, we may have been fortunate enough to have parents or older family members or friends who guided us when we were faced with situations we hadn't navigated before.

Whilst there are books on parenting that can guide us, reading the concepts and experiencing the reality can be two completely different things. We have to trust God if we believe in him, and if we don't, we must trust our instincts that we're doing the right things for our children.

It's also important to keep in mind that not all children who show the same symptoms as Marley will take an action that ends with an irreversible and a traumatic situation. Some may just be experiencing preteen or teenage hormones. Parents, do all you can to get younger children showing similar symptoms diagnosed to rule out any early stages of mental-health issues, since they are more receptive to intervention at an early age and are less likely to be stigmatised by what their peers might say.

They might fight you all the way but trust your parental instincts that you are doing the right thing. At the end of the day, you want to do all you can for your child, and whilst he or she might not understand all the whys and wherefores, you want that assurance that you did all you possibly could.

For those parents who have gone through a similar traumatic experience, I hope that what I have shared encourages you. There are many questions I still don't have answers for, but I know God is with me. Don't for one minute believe that something you did or didn't do led to your traumatic event. Don't think that God has left you or forsaken you because if you looked closely, you would realise he is the one behind the unexpected phone call or the card with encouraging words. He prompted the person who called you when you were feeling your lowest.

As I thought about what could have been going on in Marley's mind, I was questioning: Did he care for me, for his dad and his brother? Why would he put us through this trauma? I beat myself up as to how I could have missed the signs. If I don't know what signs to look for how could I know when I had missed it. These were some of the thoughts I had, and God sent friends of mine who are experienced mental-health practitioners to give me insight. Through their expertise, I clearly understand that when a person gets to the point when he decides to end his life, he's not thinking of how devastated his loved ones will feel or what the consequences of his actions will be.

For any young adults going through what Marley went through, I encourage you to seek help. There are lots of successes with therapy, and suicide is not a solution. Though you may feel like you're alone, there are many others having similar anxious thoughts. Reach out to organisations that can help you and be willing to put the coping mechanisms that they provide into practice. Also, don't reach out to people you consider online friends who really don't have the answers and probably don't even know you very well. Find someone you can trust and speak to him or her. A family member who you feel close to, or a family friend would be a good place to start. Don't take an action that will be permanent with no do-over. It's definitely not the answer.

11

Bonus Chapter: Two Aunties

My name is Catherine Thomas and I was very close to Marley. Ever since Marley was born I was one of the first people to visit Marley's mum when she had him. He was only about a few weeks old and I felt this strong bond with him. I was about five months pregnant with my first child and seeing Marley as a baby made me long for and look forward to when I would give birth to my first child.

Over the years I have been there for Marley watching him grow up to be a handsome young man. I regularly have calls with him and exchange text with him especially on his birthday. When his Auntie Rosa would visit me I was one of the aunties who would get all the sweets and biscuits that I knew his mum would not get for him but I would also soften it with educational books and stuff to balance the sweet stuff because I knew his mum would be telling me off for getting all these sweet stuff.

In 2018 when Marley's mum and dad were travelling to Malta for a wedding and they needed Marley to stay with someone rather than put the responsibility of looking after Marley on the shoulders of his brother Nathan, I was the one who Marley came to spend those four days with. It was good for him to spend some time with us as I have two children, my daughter who was four months younger than Marley and my son who was a few years younger. Marley's mum and I had agreed that there was a lot they had in common and he would not be bored.

I can recall collecting him from the train station in London since we did not live in close proximity. It was about an hour and a half train journey from their location to mine. At first he was a bit shy as he got used to his surroundings. Although he had visited, this was the first time he would be staying over and I guessed it would be new for him.

We tried not to ask too many questions but to let him feel relaxed and at home. He was soon chatting away with my son about computer and console games. As Marley was artistic he found a common ground with my daughter discussing art and how they could use art in the future after completing their education.

A day or so later he was out and about with my son, running errands to the shop. Later my children were showing me a video they had recorded of Marley pretending to me as he rang the bell to our apartment. It's a memory that will always stay with me as he was happy, very relaxed and jovial. He had definitely settled in. I remember receiving photos of Marley's mum and dad at the wedding and showing it to Marley and passing on his message that the photo was great and he loved it.

What I never knew was that this would be the last time Marley would visit and stay over at our home. I can recall having a really weird night at the hospital where I work as a midwife on the night that Marley passed. I was moving a bottle for blood transfusion and suddenly there was blood everywhere. It felt as if someone had knocked the container from my hand and the blood from the container splashed everywhere. My colleagues who were with me at the time, asked, "what happened?" It was very unusual for me to drop something.

Later in the evening of that same day, 11th December 2020 I could not believe what Marley's mum was saying to me. I would not have put Marley down as someone who was suicidal. I could not believe he was gone. How could he be gone, this young man who I had spoken to a few days earlier on his eighteenth birthday, welcoming him into adulthood. I was devastated but I had to control my emotions as I had to be strong for Marley's mum. She had lost her son in a very traumatic way and I knew if it wasn't for the strong faith she had in Jesus she would have been falling apart. I kept thinking of the previous twelve months, dancing with Marley at the wedding of his cousin in Freetown, Sierra Leone, and now he was gone.

"Lord have mercy, oh my God." These were the only words I could say when I had a call on that sad and traumatic day with Marley's mum.

"How was she not falling apart when I was feeling as if my heart was being torn from my chest?" These were some of the questions that was going through my head as I listened to her. Not knowing what to say. What could I say to someone who had just lost their son in such a traumatic way? There were no words. I had no words.

*

I am the Auntie who came from Freetown, Sierra Leone, when Marley was only five months old and lived with the family. Marley was like a son to me as I had been looking after him whilst his mum and dad were at work until he was twelve years old when I returned back to Freetown, Sierra Leone. I had been there to see him grow his first tooth, take his first step, reach key milestones like talking, first day at school, been the moderator and confidante to disagreements with friends, family and mum and dad to name a few.

I remember Marley and his family visiting me at my home in Kossoh Town. I had prepared food that they would love. I had taken very good care to ensure that there were no nuts especially groundnuts which I knew both Marley and his brother Nathan had a strong allergic reaction. They both enjoyed the food and we talked about some of the lovely memories we had shared in the UK and more recently in Gambia.

I never thought I would not see Marley as an adult with a career in Animation which was his passion, see him have his own family. I will always remember his smile, his laugh and all the good times we shared. I will hold on to my last memory of him, saying farewell at the ferry port in Aberdeen Sierra Leone as he and his family boarded the ferry to return to the UK after attending the wedding of his cousin. He had promised to visit me again in Freetown, Sierra Leone not knowing that he would not keep that promise.

My response to him when he said that was "that he should get a job, earn his own money to pay for his flight when he comes back" and his response was, yes Auntie, I will. Not knowing that this would never happen. Marley will always have a special place in my heart.

"Marley's Song"

By M. Grant

No, this is not goodbye;
It's just the start of something new.
I'll be right by your side
And hold your hand to help you through.
I'll shine a light to show you
I haven't gone away,
And I will glow within your heart
Forever and a day.
No, this is not goodbye;
It is just the start of something new.

Image of the plane I was travelling in surrounded by a rainbow.

LIVING WITHOUT MARLEY

Sequel to Marley's Memoir: The Journey to an Irreversible Action and the Aftermath

MAJENDI JARRETT

Living Without Marley

I would like to dedicate this book to my husband Trevor and my son Nathan, who gave me the permission to share their intimate thoughts and feelings of loss and grief.

I also want to thank God for the love and strength which He has given me during this difficult time and continues to give to me through friends and family, but also directly through quiet moments.

Contents

Preface...139

Introduction...141

1 Navigating a New Normal—Mum's View...143

2 Losing My Son—Dad's View...147

3 Losing My Brother—Brother's View...158

4 Let's Have Therapy—Mum's View...165

5 Marley's Legacy: Turning Lemon to Lemonade—Mum's View...172

6 Birthdays and Anniversaries—Mum's View...179

7 Getting Out There—Mum's View...188

8 Emotional Triggers—Mum's View...197

9 Overcoming Fear—Mum's View...204

10 A Beautiful Day—Mum's View...209

11 Can December Be Beautiful Again? —Mum's View...215

12 The Dark Clouds Will Get Lighter—Mum's View...221

Epilogue...225

Acknowledgments...227

Organizations That Can Help...228

Family Photos...229

Preface

A number of readers have asked at book signing events, what the next book would be about and whether I would give a voice to the other members of the family, apart from the mum who had a significant voice in the first book, *Marley's Memoir: The Journey to an Irreversible Action and the Aftermath*. It was important to give focus to the mother as she played a key role on that fateful day whilst also giving an insight into the mind of Marley, how he got to the point where he took an action which impacted those who were close to him. In this book I would like to give some insight to the thoughts and feelings of Marley's dad Trevor and his brother Nathan, to complete the picture of how they felt at the time when this event took place. I felt that it was important to share the male perspective also of loss and grief. The majority of the book gives an insight on how the family of three navigated life after this traumatic event, which covers up to the first twelve months after losing Marley.

The reader will get some understanding of the character and personality of each member of the family and how the loss of Marley impacts them. The book also covers some of the challenges the family have had to face during this time and how they try to take steps forward.

Introduction

It was a cold, cloudy December morning when I experienced the most traumatic event of my life. I had woken up quite early as I usually do to have a quiet time of prayer, reading my Bible and a devotional. I read the verse of the day and then went on to read about a woman named Martha who was in a refugee camp and had experienced the traumatic loss of her family; rebels had broken into her home and killed her husband and two of her sons whilst she and her six-month-old son were hiding. I could not begin to imagine the pain and agony she must have gone through, and I was silently asking, "God, how could you have allowed this to happen?"

Little did I know that Martha's story was preparing me for what I would be facing in a little under two hours. I was also astounded by Martha's faith and joy which the author of the devotional wanted to bring to light. Despite the tragic loss of her family, she was full of joy supporting the other refugees in the camp and ministering to them.

I finished my quiet time and proceeded to get ready for work. It was a Friday, the end of my working week. I was looking forward to some downtime, but of course I had to get through Friday first.

As I prepared for working from home, I went downstairs to boot up my laptop, turn off the outside light and open the curtains. I was surprised that the light was still on, as this indicated that Marley had not left for his paper round. I checked the back door as is my usual routine but did not realise that the door was not locked until I came back downstairs the second time. I took out the washing from the washing machine with the intention of taking the bedsheets to hang outside when I came back downstairs.

The second time round, I noticed the back door leading to the garden was not locked with the key and I assumed that my younger son had left it unlocked after leaving for his paper round early in the morning. I thought he had got up when I went back upstairs.

I went back upstairs again and finished off getting ready whilst informing my husband that the back door was unlocked and our youngest must have left it open in his rush not to be late for his paper round.

I was back downstairs for the third time and, since it was cloudy and cold, I thought I would only hang out the bedsheet and put the rest of the clothing on the clothes airer.

I grabbed the navy-blue bed sheet, opened the door leading to the garden from the utility room and saw something that no mother ever wants to see. Was I awake? I asked myself. Am I really seeing what I am seeing? Is it my imagination or is the sight in front of me real? I must be in a trance as this cannot be real. It is not true; it must be a mirage. In those few seconds, which felt like hours, I refused to accept that what I was seeing was reality. I felt I must still be asleep and having a nightmare.

I was in shock, I could not move for those few seconds and then I shouted, "Marley, Marley!" and the sound of my voice did not even seem like mine. I ran towards the mirage, which unfortunately was reality.

1

Navigating a New Normal—Mum's View

It does not matter how many sessions you have with a therapist, or books you read or what friends and family who may have gone through similar events say, your situation will always be unique to you. The way in which you navigate it will be unique to you. The pain you will feel on a daily basis will be unique to you. No one can prepare you for the mood swings or the low mood because the relationship you share with that loved one is unique to you. Don't get me wrong, you will definitely take some pointers from all what you read or sessions you attend but you will need to make it your own. By this I mean, finding what works for you. What works for you and those around you who shared in the pain and loss will be unique to each of you.

Every day will be tough, trying to make sense of it all, continuously questioning yourself. Drifting between reality and the surreal, not sure if you are sleeping, thinking that you are having a nightmare that you would wake up and realise it was not real. No relief from waking up and realising it was just a bad dream because unfortunately it is real, it did happen, this person is no longer here, and you have to live life without them.

The thought of not holding, touching, speaking with them will almost break you in two. You will question life, what is it all about? Rushing around doing things that in the face of loss becomes insignificant, you will question your ambitions and the things you had held as important or invaluable, are they worth it? These are some of the questions which will be going round and round in your head.

The time you spend on certain things will become irrelevant and you will try to reprioritise all over again. You will question the pressure you put on others to do things in a certain way, live a certain way and achieve ambitions all over again. Is it worth it? This will be the question you will ask yourself over and over again? Why? Because we do not take any of the accolades or material things we chase and work hard for when we leave this world. I remember some years back reading a book by Clayton M. Christensen, "How will you measure your life?" My manager at the time had given each of us in the team this book to guide us as we formed a new team. After reading the book it emerged that the most important thing in our lives is the relationship we have with others. The way someone felt after an encounter with us. It is not what you achieve academically or professionally that counts with those who are close to you but how you made them feel. I think a lot about how Marley felt. Had he thought that he had my time and attention?

When I walk by the shops in our local area – where our local Co-op grocery store is located – I would see the newsagents, and after a few more steps I would be by the local pizza shop, the charity shop, and finally, I would be by the chicken and chip shop. What do all these shops have in common? At one time or the other, in the previous year, Marley had been there. The newsagent would definitely get the highest score because he was there every day for his paper round. I cannot help but think that these are the same sidewalks where Marley walked just twelve months ago. Do I get emotional as these thoughts flood my mind? Of course I do. Does it make me want to run away and not experience it? No way! If anything, it takes me closer to him.

I imagine him going to the Co-op grocery store to get some crisps or a drink. I imagine the many times he went into the newsagent, not only to do his paper round but to get something. There were times when he got me a birthday card or Mother's Day card from there. Other times he got his snacks and energy drinks from there. I recall a few times when he had said, "It seems I am spending all the money I earn from the paper round in the newsagent. I need to go somewhere else." He would go somewhere else but then he would be back again spending his few pounds in the same shop where he earned it. It was very convenient. I felt the same. I have memories of Marley in this local, in this town, and although it can be emotional sometimes, I can't imagine myself being anywhere else. Definitely not. I would go to the shopping centre in our small town. I would go to the same bank, the very same one I introduced to Marley. I would go to the same supermarket and sometimes take the same route which he rode his bike after school or after the few times he had visited the game shop. It's almost as if I could see him peddling on his bike, going as fast as he could so he could get to the sanctuary of his room. There are times when I passed him on the road and even though I would toot him, he would not hear because he had his headphones on, or he was so focused on getting home that he would not hear anything else in his surroundings.

2

Losing My Son—Dad's View

My name is Trevor and I am Marley's dad. I would describe myself as a simple person. I usually say, "I don't want no fuss, no complication. I like to be in the background and not be in the spotlight." I would say that I have been like this since I was a child. I try to keep on the straight and narrow to avoid "rocking the boat", as rocking the boat means that I would be in the spotlight and I don't want to be in the spotlight, not before this event and certainly not now.

When the events of 11 December 2020 took place, it threw me completely out of my comfort zone. (If you don't know the event I am referring to, you need to read *Marley's Memoir: The Journey to an Irreversible Action and the Aftermath*.) The invasion of outsiders (by outsiders meaning the police, forensics and paramedics into our home), the questions, and the constant footfalls in and out for over two hours was unbearable. I remembered lying in bed the morning of 11 December 2020. I saw my wife going through her usual routine of getting ready for work, then she went downstairs and then back upstairs. I recalled drifting in and out of sleep. I had fallen asleep when my nap was interrupted with her on and off conversations. I vaguely heard her say something about Marley leaving the outside light on when he left for his paper round, but it all seemed far away.

Suddenly, I was abruptly brought back to full awareness by her cry: "Trevor, quickly come downstairs, it's Marley." My immediate thought was that Marley had been hit by a car as he rode out of the drive from home to go on his paper round. I remembered thinking how many times I had told him that he came out of the drive too fast without knowing who might be coming down the footpath. With a thumping heart and unsteady hands, I got out of bed as I could hear a cry from my wife, which I had never heard before. Something was seriously wrong as she kept insisting that I should hurry downstairs.

I succeeded in putting on jogging bottoms and a hoodie and went downstairs. I was not expecting to see Marley in that position. I knew immediately that he was no longer with us. I did not want to go there. At the insistence of my wife, I had no choice but to go there. In my mind, a man is expected to be brave, fearless, be the leader, take charge and be a protector. I had to do this, I could do this, is what I kept saying to myself. Later I recalled standing there in the garden looking at this sight that I did not want to see, and, in my heart, I wanted to run and hide. Unfortunately, I couldn't, I had to man up. So, with a masque of bravery to disguise my turbulent feelings I moved towards the vision on the tree. I had no choice but to do what my wife was asking: "Please get him off the tree," she said. I tried but I could not, so I asked her for scissors and then everything became surreal. There I was with my youngest son in my hands, cold as ice. I could not bear to hold him any longer so I put him down on the lawn, but I soon heard my wife saying, "Don't leave him on the grass, bring him inside." I tried telling her that he was gone but she was not listening to me, she was on the phone to the emergency services asking for an ambulance.

Together with his brother Nathan, we brought him in and laid him on the utility floor. It was devastating to see my wife lying over Marley, praying fervently for him to get up, for the life that she already knew was gone from him to fill him up. I believe in God but in my mind, I felt that this was an impossible task, even for God; or was it that my faith was not as strong as my wife's? Whilst I was contemplating this, the paramedics arrived and moved us out of the area. All I could think about was that this could not be happening. It had felt like only a few minutes ago when I was drifting in and out of sleep, enjoying the bed all to myself to be abruptly pushed into the reality of this situation. Thoughts such as Why would Marley do this? kept going through my mind. When the paramedic confirmed that Marley was gone, I was numbed. I could not cry or scream. I would have liked to break something even though I was not one to express emotions in that way. I looked at my wife and Nathan and they were in pieces. Totally heartbroken and I envied the way they could just express their feelings freely. I had to be strong for them. I was the man of the home, the protector of his family even though I was very far from feeling like a protector at the moment. I was feeling like a failure. How could I not have seen this coming? How did I miss this? Only the night before I was speaking to him about what he needed to do when he went to the bank. Marley had even posted a video clip of the press-ups his mum had encouraged him to do daily. Where were the signs that night that I missed? These were some of the questions going through my mind.

My wife was falling apart, and, in a way, I envied her that she could just let it all out whilst I felt as if I was being suffocated and could not breathe, but I kept telling myself I had to be strong. I remembered putting my arms around her, consoling her. I felt helpless but at least I could give her a hug. We sat down by the dining table just looking at each other, trying to make sense of this nightmare. During this time the police had arrived and wanted to check his room, wanted details on what happened and statements for their records. It felt like a very long day, but it all went very quickly. As much as I wanted it to be a bad dream, unfortunately it was reality. I kept being hit by this strong sense of guilt, feeling that I could have been a better father to Marley. I had not been very accommodating with Marley's ups and downs, especially in the weeks and months leading to his demise. I know I am not a very patient person. I am also very traditional in the way I see life in that children should respect elders, especially their parents. When I was growing up it was the norm to greet your parents in the morning and others around you. It was a sign of respect. These were the principles Marley and I did not agree on. Marley rebelled against these traditions, and we were always at loggerheads. It meant that our father and son relationship was not smooth running – more so in the preceding year, it was almost non-existent because I was not very accommodating of bad behaviour. Maybe it had something to do with the relationship I had with my father, but that's another story for another day.

I was constantly telling Marley off because he was not being respectful. When he wanted my help with something or the other, I was reluctant to give it to him. I remembered the evening before when Marley had asked me for a haircut, and I had ignored him. In my mind, he always chose the wrong time to ask for help. I would be available all day but the requests for a haircut were only made when I wanted to watch football, relax, or to watch something on TV. I was from the generation where children worked round the schedules of their parents and not the other way round. In my generation there was no way growing up, I would have expected my dad to work to my schedule. When I thought about having refused to cut his hair, it fills me with regret knowing that Marley was no longer here. I was gutted. I remembered lying in bed that night and saying to my wife, "Why do you think he wanted to have a haircut on Thursday night?"

"No idea," she had said.

This is one of many questions that still haunts me twelve months after the event. Honestly, I wished I could just have a good cry but unfortunately the tears were all internal, mingled with pain and guilt. I started questioning myself as I have done several times: Was I a good father? I didn't think I was. I was not the touchy, feely type like my wife. I remembered giving the boys handshakes when they were kids as a joke. My intention was to make them tough; in my mind they needed to be strong. Touchy and emotional stuff made you weak was my thinking at the time. It was okay for women to be touchy feely, I had thought. Of course, my views have since changed, but I had held on to those views for a long time and that must have shaped my relationship with Marley. When I think back, Marley just wanted someone to listen to him and give some constructive feedback, but my immediate response was always to tell him to be tough. Other times I would listen but without actually hearing him, which eventually led to Marley's withdrawal and instead going to his mother for emotional support. Besides that, I am not a natural conversationalist, I am a man of few words and trying to give words of support was well out of my comfort zone. On the other hand, if there were practical problems such as fixing a toy, or a punctured tyre on a bike, I would be the man you could call on.

The emotional stuff I left for my wife. She had a lot more comforting words to say than I did. It was this – among other reasons – that I found it hard to make the phone call to my family to tell them what had happened. What could I say? How could I start such a difficult conversation as I did not know what to say at the time. How could I tell my mum, Marley's Nan, who was almost ninety at the time, that her grandson had done this? How could I tell my sisters of this devastation? How do you even put the words together? This was taken out of my control when a friend who was driving passed the house saw all the police cars outside and called to ask me what was up? Without thinking about it I told him what had happened, and it was only afterwards I realised what I had done.

The devastating news was now out of the confines of our home and could travel like wildfire from one house to the other, from one person to the other. I was obviously not thinking clearly or it was the relief to speak to another adult male, I honestly don't know why I told him. The narrative was now out of our control and we needed to inform family and friends before they found out through the grapevine as these things had a way of travelling from one person to another. My wife was not happy and told me I had to immediately call my sister who lived close to our mum so that she could go over and break the news before one of their friends said something. I was reluctant to make the call as I did not know how she would take it. In the end my wife made the call and put it in such a way that whilst it was a shock, it was handled with the care that I knew she was capable of, and I was not. My sister was given the task of telling the rest of the family on my side as my wife had to break the news to her side of the family.

That night lying in bed I could not get to sleep. Neither could my wife because our minds and thoughts were so full of the event from the morning. It spanned the whole day, and it did not matter how much we wanted to block it out, it was like an unwanted guest which was not taking the hint to leave. In the end we gave up trying to sleep and talked. We had been told not to think about what we could have done better or how things could have been different as this sort of thinking would make us feel worse and there was nothing, we could do about it. It also stopped us from starting a blame game. I had looked at her lying there beside me, and I wondered what she was thinking. Did she think it was my fault? I would not blame her, knowing that I could have done more. I could have been more understanding of what Marley was going through as I felt that in some ways Marley was very similar to me in personality and character.

I had found school in England very challenging as a teenager. I had arrived in England at the age of fourteen from Barbados and was thrown into a very different society and culture from what I was used to. In those days there were not many black, West Indian children with strong Caribbean accents in my school, so it was a culture shock to me and my peers who treated me to some extent as if I was an alien. Fortunately for me, unlike Marley, I was really good at sport, and cricket was my passion, so I could distract myself from playing cricket and also connect with other like-minded people. These are some of the thoughts that went through my mind as we went through the preparation for the funeral and also in the days and weeks leading to the inquest. I had tried several times to share my experience with Marley when he had complained about school and not having friends. Unfortunately, on each occasion I had tried to share my experience, my words had not had the desired impact. I was more of a fixer than a talker so whatever I tried to say did not come out right and it ended with Marley saying, "It's not the same, my situation is different from yours. You cannot compare your experience with what I am going through." I thought it was best if I kept quiet and left my wife to deal with it as I knew she was better at this than I was.

I don't know how I went through the viewing and the funeral as I was reluctant to go anywhere near the funeral home, even for the meetings to discuss the arrangements. It was very hard for me, and I may be called a coward, but I just could not go there. Fortunately, the pastor went with my wife and Nathan and my sister came over to be with me whilst they were gone. I was going through the motions of getting up, fixing whatever needed to be fixed as directed by my wife and then distracting myself with football. There was a lot of distraction from football as the team I supported, Manchester United, was underperforming. I would tune into all the forums on YouTube and watch the rematch on TV and this was a good distraction for me as the day of the funeral approached. I remembered going to the viewing with the family, but it all felt unreal. I felt like a robot. I was just going through the motions, but it was not sinking in.

On the day of the funeral, it really hit me. I could not hold it back; the tears came out like a flood. I was supposed to be strong for my wife and son but as soon as we got to the church the thought of Marley lying in the coffin broke something within me. I was glad I had dark glasses to hide my tears. I could not stop the tears flowing down my cheeks even if I tried. The reality of Marley's passing really hit me. I cried all throughout the service until we got to the cemetery. Afterwards I tried to forget by watching football.

In the days that followed, I tried to discourage my wife, Jenny from watching and listening to videos of Marley on her phone, but she was not having it. She said that watching the videos helped her during her loss. It was the opposite for me as it made me really sad. I could not listen to or watch videos in those early days. There was still the inquest to come. If it was left to me, I would not have attended the opening of the inquest even though it was by a video link. After the opening of the inquest, I thought that was it. No, there was the inquest itself when we got to hear all the details read over again. It was torture going through the hearing. I really did not want to be part of it. At this time, I had been having counselling as my wife had insisted – we all needed to do. I had wanted it to be group therapy, but we were told it was best to do individual therapy and if later we needed group therapy, we could ask for it. It was not easy talking to someone about how I felt; it's not what I do. I forced myself to stick with it and succeeded in doing the eight sessions. Looking back, I think it actually helped me to be more open about how I was feeling and not to internalise everything. It helped that afterwards I could talk about it with my wife and Nathan.

The inquest was tough as this was held about three months after the event. It was about the time when I had started to adjust a bit to the new normal. Suddenly, I was plunged back into that day on 11 December and the devastating event was being recited minute by minute, hour by hour. It was very difficult for all of us. It was a very difficult hour. I tried to tune myself out and only paid attention when my wife needed to make a response, which was not very often. I honestly did not see the point of the inquest as we all knew what had happened; would it change anything? No, nothing would change; it would not bring Marley back. I was glad when it was over, and we could put it behind us. I was able to breathe easily when we got off the video call. We had hugged each other in a family group hug as we tried to put what we had heard behind us.

The following months I tried to get through some form of normalcy, but it was not easy. Everywhere I turned, I was reminded of that day. Being in the utility room where I had laid Marley when I brought him in from the garden kept giving me flashbacks. At the beginning of the year, we had a leak in the family bathroom, and it made a mess of the kitchen ceiling. We decided it would be a good time to do a bit of decorating as Marley's fingerprints were all over the walls in the hallway and the kitchen because it was his habit of always putting his fingers on the walls after tinkering with his bike. Almost every wall in our home had some imprint from Marley.

We got some paint, and it was my task to put fresh paint on the walls. In a way it gave me something to focus on, something to keep me busy and distract me from my thoughts. I could do something practical.

3

Losing My Brother—Brother's View

My name is Nathan and I am the older brother to Marley Asher Adeshino Prescott. Up until the 10 December 2020, I would say that I had had a good life. And although I had lost people who were close to me, like my granddad, nothing could have prepared me for the loss of my brother. I was not prepared. We had spent so much time together growing up, and although I knew as we entered adulthood things would change, I still felt that no matter how different we were we would always be there for each other. It was only a few months leading up to December that we were talking about when we would get married, and how our children would hang out and play together like we did as kids. Little did I know at the time that this was never going to happen. I did not realise how much I loved my brother until he was no longer there to do all the things that at the time, I had taken for granted.

I remembered waking up that morning to the cries of our mum from somewhere outside my bedroom door. "Trevor, Nathan, please come and get Marley off the tree!" I had heard her cry and so I quickly put on my jogging bottoms and ran downstairs forgetting to put on a tee shirt until I got outside and felt the cold air. As soon as I got outside, I knew something was very wrong. My whole world seemed to cave in at that moment. I could not even go near him; instead, I started pacing the length of the garden, going round and round in circles, no longer aware of the cold morning air. As tears ran down my cheeks, my hands on my head full of despair, all I was able to say was, "Why? Why? Why?" How could I have missed it? I was downstairs with him late the night before and there was nothing to indicate that he would do this. He had been sitting at the dining table eating his pizza just before I came downstairs to put the dishwasher on. For some reason we had not spoken to each other that evening, as Marley was watching something on his laptop. Without so much as a word, Marley had taken the last piece of pizza he was eating from the plate and handed it to me, to put in the dishwasher.

Later when I was in bed, I had heard him go back downstairs but did not think anything of it. Thinking back, I wondered if that was the time when these negative thoughts had gotten hold of him. If only I had gone downstairs when I heard him, would I have been a welcome distraction? I wondered. I kept beating myself up about it wondering if only? This guilt or blame would continue long after the funeral. It was at the inquest when I learned for the first time that he had said something about having suicide ideation when drinking alcohol. I kept thinking what I could have done after he had told me that he had bought alcohol on his eighteenth birthday? Was that when he had bought the alcohol, he had drunk a week later? Was there anything I could have done to stop him? At the time I had not thought much of it as I thought buying alcohol at the age of eighteen confirmed your adult status. If only I could have seen into the future. I had my parents but I felt alone; I had lost my sibling – my confidante. We talked and shared so much, yet Marley had never let on that he was having suicidal thoughts.

When I saw something on social media which I thought was funny I would share it with Marley. If I watched something on Netflix, I would tell him about it. When an artist released a single or an album I liked, I would tell him about it as we shared similar tastes. Though there was almost a four-year age gap between us, Marley understood the vibes of our generation. I lost all of this when he was no longer there. Now, I had to depend on my friends or my parents, which was not the same as when Marley was there. Marley had always been in my room, moaning about something or the other. It was not easy at times as I wanted my privacy and sometimes when he got silly, I would ask him to leave my room. How I longed for those days when he would be in my room talking nonsense about this or that. Unfortunately, those days would never come back, they were gone.

It saddens me that I did not value those days at the time and now I would never have them again. It has been very difficult going through the grieving period as it appears that everywhere I turned a young person had lost their lives, either ending it themselves or they had been the victim of a shooting or stabbing. I don't seem to be able to hide from it. It's on the news when my mum turns on the TV, it's on social media, it's everywhere. It seems that everyone has been touched by someone with some form of mental illness.

I was quite moved by the young man who was only nineteen years old and was found dead in a pond in a forest in London. It was a flashback to that rawness and freshness of loss; it brought back how I felt in those early days and reminded me that although it felt as if I was still in the same space I was actually moving forward, though very slowly. I did not want to think about the Christmas after Marley passed or the preparation for the funeral. The funeral itself was too hard. I sometimes feel embarrassed when I think of how I lost it at the graveside. The reality of it all hit me whilst I was standing by the grave, seeing the coffin descending, knowing that my baby brother who I had known for all his eighteen years was no longer with us. I could not control my legs. All of a sudden, my legs became wobbly, and I could barely keep myself upright. I was sobbing uncontrollably, and I did not care who was looking at me or heard me. I was glad my mum led me away from it all so that I could no longer see the coffin in the grave.

No one can prepare you for the loss of someone close to you. When the hearse had arrived at our house it was my mum who was falling apart. I was the one who consoled her all the way to the church for the service, and now the table had turned around. She was the one who consoled me. Afterwards, it was a relief to get home and just be with my parents. Knowing that we had gone through the hardest part was like a weight off my shoulders, although nothing could be compared to that Friday morning. Neither the funeral nor the inquest could compare to that terrible Friday morning when our world was turned upside down. That Friday would forever be imprinted in my mind, and the smell of that day would sometimes come vividly to me. Helping my dad carry Marley inside – his wet clothes, which were soaked from a bit of rain and probably his body fluids – will stay with me forever.

My first birthday without Marley was much better than I had thought. Mum decided that we should have McDonald's since it was a Saturday, and we should watch video recordings of happier times with Marley when we had gone on holiday to Barbados and Florida. She wanted to transfer some of these recordings from a camcorder to her phone, so she would have easy access to it. I was the person delegated with this task. My dad and I had thought at first that it would be difficult to watch the videos of Marley. My first thoughts were this is not how I wanted to spend my birthday. It turned out to be very comforting as we went back to the days when we were very young, on our first family holiday in Barbados, my dad's place of birth. I remembered that holiday as if it was yesterday, staying up later than our usual bedtime, meeting family for the first time and having lots of fizzy drinks and junk food at our disposal. Also being able to see the younger Nathan and how forward I was compared to now, I thought I was a bit more reserved now than I was in my early years. In the end I was able to transfer quite a few memories from the camcorder to mum's phone and in the process refreshed my memory of the good times I had with Marley.

When I reflect on those early days after the funeral, one of the things I would recommend to anyone who has suffered the tragic loss of a loved one is counselling. Just to talk to someone else, especially someone you don't know, can be comforting. At first, I was very reluctant to talk to a stranger about personal stuff. After some persuasion from mum, I gave in. My intention was to try one session and if I felt uncomfortable, I would withdraw from further counselling. My first session was good, and I was given some coping mechanism which helped me to deal with the pain and loss. I attended all eight sessions and also put in for a further two as the therapist advised me, I would need more sessions after the inquest. The therapist also helped me to think about how I would like to remember Marley. I had several ideas and one of which I would take forward in the coming months.

It was around that time when mum first told me about the foundation she wanted to start as a legacy to Marley and return to the book that she had started writing in 2019. I thought it was great that she had these two ideas to focus on as she had been really down. Whilst she had the desire to look deeper into Marley's phone to get some answers and research for the book, I had no desire to dig deeper into Marley's past. My dad and I had decided not to look deeper into what Marley was thinking at the time and why he did what he did. Maybe in a way I might be called a coward, but I did not want to come across something that would be upsetting for me. Mum had shared with me some of her discoveries after accessing Marley's phone. She said it gave her some understanding of Marley's state of mind. I had also kept quite a few of the WhatsApp voice messages which Marley had sent to me over time. I had forwarded the messages to her since she said it would also give her some clarity. Unfortunately, around this time, I kept getting a type of vertigo which kept me in bed for two to three days at a time. It was very worrying for me and my parents as we did not understand what the root cause was. I would be fine one minute and the next minute I was unsteady on my feet due to bouts of dizziness which made me feel nauseous. I had four episodes in the space of ten months before we identified a root cause. It was difficult for all of us at this time, especially since we were still recovering from the unexpectedness of Marley's passing and we did not have the strength to deal with another unknown.

4

LET'S HAVE THERAPY—MUM'S VIEW

One thing I would recommend after a tragedy or traumatic event is counselling. It can be very daunting talking to a stranger about deep and personal things which you might not even be able to discuss with someone who you are close to. I was not very keen on the idea when it was suggested to me by friends and family and others who had walked the road I was on. I decided to give it a try and also encouraged my family to do the same. There was reluctance from Trevor and Nathan, which was not surprising. If I was finding it hard to make that first step, I knew that Trevor and Nathan would find this even more difficult. I knew if we were going to do this then it would be down to me to make the calls and link up the respective therapist to each of us.

I focused on Trevor as he was the one who seemed to have kept all his emotions inside and I knew that although he was not saying it, he was hurting. Every night before going to sleep, if you could call snippets of shut eye here and there sleep, he would open up a bit. I was able to get some idea of the unfounded guilt and blame he had harboured. He had said a few times that "he was not a good father and that he could have done more for

Marley". I would stop him immediately from going down that guilt ridden trap. "There are things that you are good at and there are things that I am good at," I would say. We were together in this. As parents we were not in competition; if I did something for Marley it was for both of us, and if he did something for Marley, then it was for both of us. Whilst I had been good at the emotional and touchy-feely stuff, he had been quite good at the physical, action driven stuff.

Trevor was the first one to start therapy sessions. I had paired him with someone who I hoped would push him a bit out of his comfort zone and get him to open up. After his first session, he said it was helpful. I could hear him laughing when I walked past the bedroom; I thought if he had the right person, he would find it beneficial. I was not sure if he would attend all eight sessions, but I was happy that he had started and seemed to be getting something from it. After three sessions he was given some exercise to channel his grief, which he had to do in between sessions. At first, he was not sure what the benefit was, but I encouraged him to do it and gradually he started to get something out of it.

With Nathan it took a bit more effort to get him to agree to see a therapist as he did not see what the point of it was. He kept saying he was fine and did not think that the sessions would add any value. After trying different tactics, he was still unwilling to engage, so I used my trump card. I told him that refusing therapy reminded me of Marley not wanting to engage in counselling. I was not below using any tactics I could to get him at least to try it. It was in the same way he did not want to get help because he thought he did not need it. This actually did the trick. We agreed that he would at least do one session and if he did not want to do any more, I would not force him. Again, I was very fortunate that the therapist I had paired him with, was someone who could relate to him. His sessions were Saturday mornings, which worked well for him and after the first session he agreed to have another one. It was also helpful that it was a phone call and not a video call, like Trevor and I had engaged in. Nathan could talk to her almost as if he was speaking to someone he knew because he could not see her.

When I had my first session with my therapist, I realised that she was best suited to me. She would ask a question and then allow me the time to respond, which would result in me giving her far more than I realised. She would make notes and then asked me a further question about what I had said. In this way she allowed me to open up. Around this time, I was finding it very hard to sleep for longer than three hours without waking up. If I went to bed around midnight, I would still wake up between 1.30 and 2 o'clock in the morning, and I would find it really hard to go back to sleep as I would be thinking of Marley. My thoughts would take me back to the timeline of what he was doing around that time on that fateful morning. I would eventually go back to sleep, but I would wake up again around 3am and would stay awake until 4 or sometimes 5 o'clock in the morning.

The first few nights after the event, a friend recommended herbal sleeping pills. I took the minimum dose, but it did nothing, I still woke up at the same time. I took the maximum dosage, and it did nothing, I still woke up at the same time. I stopped taking the pills and around this time the nurse from the doctor's surgery reached out and asked if there was anything we needed. I said I could not sleep and had not had a good sleep since the event. I was prescribed a different herbal sleeping pill which also was non-effective. When I shared my sleeping pattern with my therapist, she gave me an insight into why I was waking up around this time. According to her theory, I was trying to save Marley from what he did. This was based on the fact that when I woke up, I would think about all the actions and steps he took; it was as if I could see and hear him walking down the stairs, opening the door leading to the garden, taking the chairs to the bottom of the tree, and then testing for height. These thoughts kept going round and round in my head and when I shared this with my therapist, she said it was the motherly desire to protect and save Marley. I had this strong desire in my subconscious to stop him from going through with his action and this was what would cause me to wake up around the time he had taken those steps, because in my subconscious, I still thought I could prevent what had happened.

In one of my sessions, I also shared that if someone should knock on the door who resembled Marley and told me that he was the real Marley I would believe it. She told me that it was that protective nature of not wanting to believe and accept that Marley could have taken this irreversible action.

Whilst my therapist really encouraged me to talk about the traumatic event, Trevor's therapist focused a lot on his relationship with his parents and siblings. She wanted him to discuss his upbringing – the first fourteen years of his life in Barbados and then his relationship with his children and his wife. It is quite interesting that she focused on these aspects as it was what he needed but did not realise it. He was constantly self-reflecting on his relationship with Marley, and what he could have done better, and so it was essential for him to reflect on the affinity he had with his dad and whether that had any bearing on his relationship with his sons.

After our sessions, sometimes, we would share some parts of our therapy sessions and he would say, "I wonder why she asks me about what happened?"

"Does your therapist ask you about your upbringing and relationships?" I would respond.

"No, my therapist was more focused on what happened and how that has affected my sleep."

He thought he was not getting anything out of it because the discussion was more focused on his early life, growing up and going to school. I would tell him that the therapist was probably trying to find similarities to his relationships and school life with Marley's. From his viewpoint he did not think he got much out of it, but I thought differently as it helped us as a family to talk more openly.

I recall one occasion telling my therapist that the things I thought would make me emotional had no effect, whilst the normal or ordinary things were what usually set me off. She gave me a really good insight into this; the normal or ordinary things are no longer normal or ordinary because Marley is no longer part of it. Things such as preparing my porridge for breakfast or putting croissants in the oven would set me off because Marley was usually part of that routine. We would both be competing for the microwave or the oven and most of the time he would beat me to it so that I had to wait for him before I did my bit. Without him, it was like a new normal and I was finding it hard to navigate this new normal as he was no longer a part of it. This was setting me off. Familiar songs from church would also set me off as I would get flashbacks of taking Marley and Nathan to church and singing these songs. On the other hand, going to the cemetery and putting flowers on the grave, liaising with the funeral masons for the headstone did not act as a trigger. It was confusing for me. I had sixteen sessions in total and whilst it was beneficial, I was glad when it ended. Whilst talking about the traumatic event was helpful, it was also very draining to me emotionally. I would finish therapy and have a really good cry. Maybe that was a good thing as it gave me the outlet to let it all out.

I was still struggling with my sleep. After the insight from the therapist, I succeeded in sleeping through until 3 o'clock in the morning. Around this time, I had access to the Campaign Against Living Miserably (CALM), one of the sources of support my employer had made available to me. I had three sessions with the sleep coach which helped. Some of the suggestions were breathing exercises which a friend of mine had also shared with me. When I woke up, I would do the breathing exercise and it would calm my thoughts and help me to go back to sleep. Another was listening to the different sounds or stories being read but these were sometimes too short, and it would finish before I had gone back to sleep. I decided to try going to sleep with the radio on as I discovered that when I slept with a background noise and woke up during the night, I could easily go back to sleep as I would not start thinking about the event of December 2020. Waking up to silence caused me to immediately start thinking of what had happened and then I found it hard to go back to sleep. My sleeping pattern improved after trying this.

Trevor was finding it hard to sleep through the night as well. His sleep was not as erratic as there were times when I would wake up and I would lie for hours listening to him breathing in and out. His problem was that when he woke up, he did not feel rested. He was sometimes more tired than before he had slept. He would go to sleep with his earphones on, listening to some comedy on YouTube and when he woke up, he would still be tired.

Nathan's sleeping pattern was messed up also but in a different way. He usually went to bed late but because of everything that had happened, he found it hard to fall asleep until the early hours of the morning. When he was not working it was alright but when he started working it was a challenge to get up for work. Fortunately, he had a late start, so he did not have to get up early in the morning.

5

MARLEY'S LEGACY: TURNING LEMON TO LEMONADE—MUM'S VIEW

As a mother or even as parents we have ambitions for our children. What they will achieve, what careers they will have, what they will do in life, who they will marry and how they will raise their children. It is very difficult to lose someone who was physically sick, more so someone who was physically healthy and had no known illness. When tragedy strikes, you feel that you are left with nothing; all the dreams and hopes you had for that person are gone with them and it feels that you are left with nothing except this pain and loss. This sense of pain and loss can be felt in different ways; you may become depressed and stay in that period of grief; you could be in denial and stay in that state of unbelief or you could try to channel the ambition you had for that person in a positive action. I have gained more understanding why people who had suffered a great loss become motivated to channel their efforts into a good cause.

I can totally relate to why they do it. I totally get it now. I remember a few hours after we had shared with close family the traumatic loss of Marley and someone close to me said, "When life gives you lemons, you make lemonade." At the time I had no idea what that meant. I knew it was about taking something bad and turning it into something good, but I was steeped in grief and could not see beyond that. How could I? My baby was no longer with us. A few days later someone else said something similar to me. Exactly a week later I woke up in the morning and I had this strong impression that I would start something in Marley's name as a legacy to him. It was very clear in my mind that it would be connected to art or animation or both, which he loved, and it would also be connected to anxiety and social disorder, which he suffered from. I wrote my thoughts down and decided I would look into this later, after the burial.

A month or so after the funeral I spoke to someone from a local charity who was giving me support to navigate the aftermath of this traumatic event. We had calls once every two weeks. She had asked me how I would like to remember Marley and I had shared with her what my thoughts were. She encouraged me to speak to the CEO of an organisation which supported young people who had similar issues to what Marley had. Around the same time, I had started a conversation with the principal of Marley's former secondary school. It was becoming much clearer how I could turn this "lemon into lemonade". I did not want to do just a one-off activity. It had to have longevity, so I had to think and plan carefully. Although making a one-off activity such as a bench in the park or donating to a charity that cares for young people with anxiety would have been good, in my opinion it was not enough. It was not what I was looking for. After speaking to the CEO of the organisation it became clear that they would play an important part in whatever I did for Marley's legacy.

I shared my thoughts with Trevor and Nathan as they needed to be involved, but in what capacity was not very clear at the time. I had a few more calls with the CEO who linked me up with other people in her organisation who had set up charities in the past. As I was not qualified in psychological therapies, I knew that I would need to involve people who were qualified to work directly with the target beneficiaries. I could create a platform to raise the provision and provide aid for this. Marley's Child Trust Fund had been given to me as the next of kin and whilst I could have just given it to any organisation associated with young people, I held on to it as it made sense that it should be part of the startup funds for his legacy. I had never set up a charity before or been a trustee for a charity, so I had a lot of reading to do and research to ensure that I was doing the right thing.

I remember in those early days reaching out to sources which I thought would give some directions. Sources such as my local bank had no idea what was involved in opening an account for a charitable organisation. I knew I needed an account for the charity, but they could not advise on setting up the charity. They pointed me to the Citizens Advice Bureau (CAB), who pointed me to the Charity Commission website. Of course, I knew the website was there with a lot of information which at first reading did not make sense, hence the reason why I was reaching out to someone who I could speak to. I thought that was my first realization that this was not going to be easy. I pushed through because anything worth doing is never easy. There was a lot of information on the charity commission website, and I started breaking it down into parts to make sense of it. One of the contacts from the CEO helped me to understand the different types of charities and how they could be set up. This was just a one-hour call, but it gave me so much insight on what I wanted and what I did not want.

I was now clear on what I wanted, and I had to identify who would be involved. It was a given that Nathan, Marley's brother, would be part of this. We brainstormed on who the other likely trustees would be. There were one or two people who had already registered an interest to be involved if I decided to do something. There were others who I believed should be part of it because they had been part of Marley's life from the very beginning: his godmother Jennifer, and his cousin Emma. I reached out to the potential trustees outlining what the charity would be set up for and to let me know if they wanted to be part of it. It was not enough that I wanted them to be part of it, they needed to want it also.

On acceptance we had a meeting in which I set out what the charity would do and how we would achieve this. I also shared what funds we had to start off with but of course we needed to generate more if we were to succeed in our objectives. I knew even before we brainstormed that there would be a charity fund-raising walk in Marley's name around the time of his birthday, but exactly what that would look like still needed to be defined. We brainstormed on other ideas and one of the trustees put forward an idea to lose 7kg during the seventh month of Marley's passing. She had an objective to raise seven hundred pounds, and, in the end, she raised over eight hundred pounds. We also started the process of registering the charity which would be named Marley's Aart Foundation. This was a tedious process and after filling all the forms and getting all the signatures from trustees and witnesses, I submitted the application on the website only to be advised two weeks later that the application did not qualify as the starting funds were below five thousand pounds. I had somehow missed this important point that in order to register the charity, then, it should have generated an income of five thousand pounds. It was a setback but did not stop us from moving forward to opening the charity account, creating the website, and starting the planning for the fundraising walk in December 2021.

The next obstacle was creating the JustGiving account. I wanted to create an account in the charity's name, but it was not possible as we were missing the elusive charity registration number from the charity commission because the charity was not yet registered. After trying different avenues, the best which was open to us was doing a crowd funding page for the fundraising walk. At this time, I had also been advised it would be good to be recognised by the Inland Revenue, so I had to fill more forms, read through lots of information on the internet to get the recognition from Her Majesty's Revenue and Customs (HMRC). In December, just after the first Marley's Memory 8km Walk, we received the confirmation letter from the HMRC that the foundation was now a recognised charity for Inland Revenue purposes. There was still the charity registration to do but this needed to be done once we had raised five thousand pounds or more from the fundraising walk which by this time, we had agreed to name Marley's 8KM Memory Walk. We successfully achieved the minimum amount to register the charity. This was a key milestone as it meant we had met a key criterion for the application for the registration. In July 2022, after a lot of backwards and forwards with the case worker at the charity commission, Marley's Aart Foundation was registered as a charity in England and Wales. This was a victorious day for us as trustees. We had spent hours in preparation, meetings and of course reading and signing documents to ensure that we understood and were aligned on how we should run the charity and meet the needs of its objectives. I was very happy we had done this by ourselves without paying for services to provide guidance and direction on how to register a charity as all the money saved could go towards helping young people.

Whilst we were setting up the charity and also preparing for the fundraising walk, I also started working with Marley's secondary school. I wanted Marley's Aart Foundation to play some part in making school life more comfortable and bearable for children who were transferring from the primary school to secondary school. The initial plan was to fund buddy benches inscribed with Marley's name which would be put in the playground where the new intake of year seven children aged 11–12 could connect and make new friends. I did not want other children to go through what Marley had endured throughout his secondary school life. It was a great day when we succeeded in having the first one installed at Queensbury Academy in Dunstable, UK, in October 2021.

I mentioned earlier that I wanted Trevor and Nathan to be involved in the charity. Whilst I had the need to channel my pain and loss in this way, for Trevor it was different. He preferred to support without being a trustee of the charity. Nathan on the other hand, is a co-founder and a trustee. At first, he found it difficult to understand where he fitted in apart from being Marley's brother. He did not want to be involved just because Marley was his brother. He found his calling when we realised that we needed a website for the public to visit and understand what Marley's Aart Foundation is about. He got a lead from one of my colleagues and from that he created the website. It was not straightforward but he kept at it until the website was created and functional, which you can check out at www.marleysaartfoundation.com. He soon realised that his role is being the creative trustee as he created the Instagram page for the foundation and manages it. He also successfully identified the company who would produce the vests worn for Marley's 8KM Memory Walk all over the world.

6

Birthdays and Anniversaries—Mum's View

Some of the hardest things to accept after you lose someone are the birthdays and anniversaries that are celebrated together. Every anniversary becomes a reminder of the difference between now and how it was before. The first Christmas was very difficult. We had to start a new tradition with the three of us and after navigating it, we felt very proud of ourselves that we would be able to face any of the others to come. Well, that was what I thought. New Year was always low key, so I did not expect it to be emotional. Sometimes it's what you don't expect that really hits you.

The first of these birthdays was Nathan's in February. I was not looking forward to it because I did not know how any of us would feel. It so happened that one of my nieces was getting married on the same day in Sierra Leone. Although I could not be there in person, I planned to join virtually since they had catered for family and friends who could not physically be there because the pandemic was still in force and travelling was not back to normal. Whilst Nathan's birthday was not a significant milestone like the previous year, I still wanted us to make it special. I decided we would bring Marley into it by watching the video recordings we had done when we went on holiday. I also wanted Nathan to transfer these videos to my phone and then to my laptop, so I had back-up in case anything went wrong with my phone. I soon realised that these were precious memories which I did not want to lose, hence the backups.

Trevor and Nathan were not keen on reliving these memories as they thought it would be too emotional. I disagreed of course and they agreed to humour me. After watching a few of the ones we took in Barbados about fourteen years ago, they soon got into it and realised that it was not as emotional as they had first thought. The videos took us back to times when we had had a good time with Marley, what they were into as children and also some petty sibling squabbles which made us laugh. It was refreshing to relive those moments and we got lost in memory lane. Even though Trevor had been reluctant he soon got into it as he was the one who had done most of the recording. We laughed at the recordings I had done, as you could easily tell the difference because mine were all over the place.

The day was progressing nicely, and we felt that Marley was with us even though not physically. We could hear his four-year-old voice in the videos taken in Barbados and then his eleven-year-old voice in the videos taken in Florida. Later we ordered a takeaway from MacDonald's. I ordered what Marley would usually order, a Big Mac, although I stuck with a single rather than a double, which was his favourite. After the meal, which was a lot and I would not make a habit of ordering on a regular basis, I connected on zoom with family and friends for my niece's wedding. It was great to be part of it even though it was virtual, and it also helped to make Nathan's birthday memorable for all the right reasons.

The next celebration was Mother's Day, and I was dreading it as whilst I was preparing myself for an emotional breakdown it might turn out to be just an ordinary day. It was not that Marley was in the habit of doing something special on Mother's Day for me, it was more that he would not be there. I need not have worried as it turned out to be a very good day. There was an inspiring message from my Pastors in the service, there were cards from unexpected sources and also Nathan and Trevor went out of their way to make it special. I had Marley's card from 2020, which I would always treasure so that came out from the drawer and was placed with the others. Nathan kept asking me how I was and making sure that I was not feeling too sad. When I look back on that day it definitely went better than I expected.

I was feeling stronger. We were all feeling stronger. We had navigated a birthday, Mother's Day and also Easter with no setbacks. The next milestone in my opinion was Trevor's birthday in July. I thought if Nathan's birthday had gone alright, then why not the same for Trevor. You can imagine how blindsided I was when the month of June turned up and I fell apart. I was not expecting it. Every eleventh day of the month I had been lighting a candle for Marley, posting messages on my WhatsApp status to mark the day. I was also putting flowers on his grave at the cemetery, either the weekend before the eleventh or the weekend after. This was my new routine; I was expecting June to be no different. When I woke up on Saturday 5 June it felt like any other Saturday. I had my quiet time with the Lord followed by prayer time with my close family friend who had been supporting me since Marley passed. After this it was a day to deep clean the house and as usual, I put on gospel songs on my iPad connected to a speaker and I was singing and praising as I did the cleaning when suddenly it dawned on me that on this day, six months ago, was the last time the four of us had cleaned the house as a family of four.

I was suddenly hit with this overwhelming sadness. It was as if I was back in December, the last Saturday Marley was with us. Everything we had done that day, including the argument Marley and I had had when I told him to spend some of his birthday money on clothes that he needed and not on junk food. I was thinking to myself, how did I miss this? I checked the calendar in the kitchen and then realised that the month of June had the exact dates and day as December 2020, except that December had 31 days whilst June had 30 days. I had been told by someone that when the eleventh fell on the exact day when the event happened, it would be tough, so I had checked earlier in the year and knew that the 11 June would be on a Friday. But this was where I stopped. It did not occur to me that for the eleventh to be a Friday all the days leading before that date and after would be exactly the same as December. I was prepared in my mind for Friday the 11 June but not for the days before or the days after. What made it worse was having the knowledge of what actions Marley was putting in place without knowing the impact this would have on us for the rest of our lives. Also knowing that the 5 December was when he had made a significant purchase.

I continued cleaning but I was crying silently until I got a phone call from another good friend. She was calling to check on me and the moment she asked how I was, I fell apart and started sobbing. She immediately thought the worst had happened as it was only six months ago; I was giving her devastating news. Her immediate assumption was that something terrible had happened. She started praying but at the same time asking me what was wrong. "Is Trevor, okay?" she asked. "What about Nathan?" she continued to question me. I continued to cry, but informed her they were both fine, only struggling to come to terms with our loss and the dates that would prove to be a constant reminder. She breathed a sigh of relief that nothing terrible had happened and continued to pray with me. After praying for me she asked if I would like to go grocery shopping with her when I had finished cleaning. I was not too sure about it as I just wanted to be left alone. Sometimes it is good to be left alone but other times it is best if you are surrounded by others who care for you. On this occasion I wanted to be left alone but I would be open to company later. We agreed that she would stop by later on her way to the supermarket and if I was up to it, I would go with her.

I needed the space to think and grieve, let out some of the pain and hurt as I was feeling that piercing pain in my chest all over again and I knew I could not just bottle it up. Trevor and Nathan had noticed that I was crying and the difference in our process made itself very clear again. They were both asking why I was crying. I wanted to scream and shout, "Really, you don't know that today, exactly six months ago, Marley was ordering a rope to end his life. How could you ask me why I am crying. Where have you been the last six months?" What I now realise is the capacity I have to store and recall all these details is a unique quality I have and they don't.

I did not scream or shout but something in my expression must have caused something to click in their brains, as Nathan immediately said, "It's Marley you are thinking of."

I nodded as I could not say anything. He gave me a hug. We had earlier intended to go over to visit the family, but I was not in the mood to face anyone outside of our family. Nathan was torn between going with his dad and staying with me. I was feeling much more composed by this time and told them I would be alright. It would be good for me to be by myself. They were reluctant but, in the end, they left me alone. I sat outside in the garden and listened to music. I had discovered CeCe Winans' album around this time and I had it on loop whilst I relived 5 December 2020. The song "Believe for It" (written by CeCe Winans, Dwan Hill, Kylie Lee and Mitch Wong) was my favourite:

> *You are the way when there seems to be no way,*
> *We trust in You God, You have the final say.*
> *Move the immovable*
> *Break the unbreakable*
> *God, we believe*
> *God, we believe for it*

An hour or so later, I was feeling better.

Another friend called me, and we chatted for about an hour or so. She had lost her dad and her brother within days apart. We encouraged each other and I felt I needed a change of scenery and the offer from my friend

Jacqueline to go grocery shopping would be a welcome change. Whilst my faith in God is very strong, I know I could not have survived without my army of friends and family. There was always someone there if I needed to talk or if I needed someone to go somewhere. Later I would check the calendar for the coming years to identify what other months had dates and days similar to December 2020. I wanted to be prepared. The rest of June was not as devastating. Although each day leading to the eleventh was playing vividly in my mind, I was more prepared after Saturday 5 June.

Trevor's birthday came round in July, and we had a quiet day. Trevor is not one to make any fuss, or so he kept telling me. I know that if we did not recognise the day he would feel put out. I know this from the odd comments he drops now and again. We had a nice meal and gave him presents. He got two fish for the outside fishpond, and it kept him busy acclimatising them to their new surroundings and a new family of fish.

September was not far away, and it would be my birthday. It was the first time I had not been looking forward to it. Whilst Trevor was not a big fan of celebrating his birthday, I was the opposite. I always planned to do something nice even if it was just taking the day off from work so I could talk to friends and family far and wide. This year I did not know how I would feel on the day. I wanted to make a conscious effort to have a good day and to start creating new memories. My birthday was on a Thursday and I would be having tea with two ladies from my church on the Friday, the day after my birthday. This was definitely something to look forward to. I had taken the Thursday and the Friday off work so I could have a long weekend break. I thought because I had been expecting my birthday to be difficult, I had subconsciously been preparing myself.

I felt no different on the morning of my birthday. Trevor and Nathan made sure that I did not feel emotional. From the morning when I got up until I went to bed there were calls and texts and friends stopping by with gifts and flowers and cards and cakes. Trevor had an urgent family matter that he needed to attend to, and although he was reluctant to leave us alone, I encouraged him to go and assured him that Nathan and I would be fine. Besides, we had our friends who would either visit or call to speak with me.

The day and days after were memorable. I received lots of texts and calls of good wishes and blessings from all over the world. Besides the flowers, cakes, gifts and cards from friends and family there were invites for dinners and lunches. I really felt cared for and continued to thank everyone who did not give me a moment to be sad, especially Nathan. Don't get me wrong, I did think of Marley as there is not a day that goes by without me thinking of him. He would be forever ingrained in my thoughts.

Our wedding anniversary which followed in October was uneventful. After previous birthday celebrations I was not expecting any unexpected triggers to make me emotional. My sadness was borne out of the change in weather and the seasons as we were now in autumn and approaching winter. The days were shorter and the nights longer and I was not looking forward to it. Added to this I had all the timeline imprinted in my mind of the intense research he was doing around this time in 2020. I realised that I would have to get used to this time of the year for different reasons. Before, it was just the fact that it got quite cold and dark; now there was the added element of Marley not being here.

7

GETTING OUT THERE—MUM'S VIEW

Although I had previously told the family that we would not be doing anymore vacations when we had come back from Sierra Leone after all the stress I had gone through, it did not extend to short breaks. After the last seven months and the lockdowns we had endured, I was keen to go away somewhere; anywhere within the UK was good as I could not contend with all the bureaucracy of travelling abroad. I knew this would not be an easy subject to broach with Trevor and Nathan, and as much as they would have liked a change of scenery, there were other things to think about. How would it feel stepping out as a family of three instead of the usual four? I can tell you. It is hard. No sugarcoating it, but life had to go on. As much as Trevor and Nathan did not want to do it, I strongly felt that we needed it. We had been cocooned in our home for a long time and we needed a change of scenery. I knew I would have my work cut out as Trevor was not keen on driving far.

I started by researching where we could go that would be far enough but would be manageable to drive to and back within the day. At this time I was not thinking of an overnight stay as I thought it would be a hard sell with Trevor. I thought a zoo would be good. We enjoyed going to the zoo when the children were younger so that could be a good place to start. I also thought somewhere located by the seaside would be good as we all loved it when we had gone on beach holidays, although it is not the same in England. With these two things in mind, I started doing my research on the internet. Not long after I started searching, I came across Africa Live Zoological Reserve in Lowestoft, Suffolk. It was over a two-hour drive. We could go the scenic route, stop on the way and back, which would take about a five-hour round trip. I told Trevor about it, and he thought it would be better if we stayed overnight instead of doing the round trip on the same day. I was pleasantly surprised when he said to do overnight. This was perfect as it meant we could visit more places. I also shared with Nathan how he felt about visiting the zoo I had identified and staying overnight. He was also fine with it, especially since he had been confined to the house the week before we went due to catching the coronavirus.

I decided to do more research on what other places we could visit, hotels we could stay at and restaurants where we could eat. This was great. I had something to plan: what we needed to take with us, the route we needed to take, when to leave and what we were able to take with us. After getting the tickets for the zoo I also got tickets for Sea Life in Great Yarmouth as I had decided we would stay at a hotel in Great Yarmouth so we could take a walk by the seaside. If we were going to see the animals at the zoo on land it made sense also to see the creatures in the water. After I had booked everything, I shared it with Nathan. He got excited as it awakened his childhood memories of family outings of going to Whipsnade Zoo.

On the morning of our trip to the zoo, we got up early so we could get to our first destination in good time. It was only an overnight stay, but I had packed a lot of things. I was not taking any chances. I had packed everything from painkillers to beddings, from cutleries to mugs, as I was not too sure about the hotel we were staying at. Most hotels in Great Yarmouth were booked up and there were hardly any rooms available in a good location by the seafront. Trevor and Nathan were wondering why I had so many bags but later on they would thank me for having the insight to take some of the things which they were making fun of.

When we set off it was a nice day. The outward journey was good as we followed the Satnav and soon, we were picking up signs for the zoo. On the way, we drove past some young women who had been desperate for the bathroom, and it was obvious that they could not find one as they were crouched on the side of the road. It amused us that this was something that was common to us all: when you've got to go, you've got to go. They were desperate for the bathroom. It's one of the reasons why Trevor does not like doing long journeys as there are not many places where you can stop to use the toilet, especially if it's not on the motorway. Maybe investing in a portable toilet is something one should consider for long journeys.

Not too long after, we arrived at the zoo, and it turned out to be a lovely day. The zoo was not too full, and we could find a parking space and move around easily. We were able to catch some of the feeding times for the animals and listen to some of the background stories. What really amused us was the lions. There were about five of them and all they did whilst we were there was sleep. They are supposed to be the "Kings of the Jungle," yet they were more "Sleep of the Jungle." They would get up, move a couple of feet forward and drop back to the grass like a sack of potatoes. Nathan was able to do a short clip of one of the lions doing just that. It was simple but it was fun. My favourite thing to do was watch the meerkats; there were loads of them. In real life they appeared so much smaller than watching them on TV. It was great seeing how they chased each other, how carefree they were. Although Marley crossed my mind a few times whilst we were at the zoo and we did say that he would have enjoyed it, we were not sad or emotional. It takes a lot of courage and determination to do something for the first time without a loved one who has passed but when you do it, it feels very freeing.

When we left the zoo, we drove to the hotel. It should have taken us twenty minutes but took about an hour because of road works and diversions. The hotel was worse than I had expected but there was nothing we could do about it. We checked in and settled into our room. It was a suite to sleep up to four people. I soon realised once we got into the suite that my bedding would be needed as well as the cutlery and mugs. Trevor and Nathan assured me that it was only for one night and we could manage. We relaxed a bit then we stepped out for dinner. I had booked a restaurant with high ratings for good fish. We found our way there and then we were faced for the first time with being seated at a table for four when there were now only three of us. Trevor and I usually sat facing Nathan and Marley. For the first time we had an empty chair in front of us and it was hard for all of us but more so for me. Although the last dinner we had at a restaurant with Marley was for Nathan's twenty-first birthday and he was miserable, I would rather have had him there with us sulking or miserable than not at all. That may sound selfish, but it was hard knowing that he would never share another dinner with us in this life. The meal was lovely, the atmosphere was good, but it did bring home for me that Marley was no longer with us.

After dinner we walked back to the hotel and that night I dreamt about Marley. He was happy in the dream which is how he is when I have dreams of him. I believe it is one of the ways God reassures me that Marley is fine, as every dream I have had of him he has been happy and, in the dream, we would have a wonderful time together to the extent that when I woke up, I am filled with joy. I had not felt sad. I shared with Trevor and Nathan what I had dreamt, and they said it was his way of comforting me after being sad at dinner. We went for a walk by the beach before going to the Sea Life Centre. We saw penguins and different types of sea creatures at the centre before making our way home. Our journey back was not as uneventful as we missed our turning on the motorway and drove for about ten minutes on the new road which the Satnav could not pick up because it was not up to date. It added an additional thirty minutes to our journey home. Trevor was not amused, and I knew it would take a lot of convincing to get him to go on another long journey. That would be a battle for another day.

A few weeks after our overnight stay in Great Yarmouth, Trevor and I had an invitation to a sixtieth birthday party with an overnight stay. There is one thing I have accepted over the years being married to Trevor is that he is a homebody. If he had his way, he would not go anywhere because his favourite pastime is chilling at home. When I broached the subject of going to this birthday celebration his first reaction was to reject it because he was not in a party mood, and he did not think he would feel like it on the day. If there is one thing, I have learnt in the last eight months is to be persistent. There was no way I would let him dwell on how he was feeling and not try to get him out of that funk. It was for this reason that since we lost Marley, I always found a project around the house for him to get his teeth into because his way of showing that he cares is by fixing things and taking care of any DIY project especially since he retired. For Nathan it was all about exercise, going to the gym was his passion so when he did not go for two to three days, I knew he was in a funk, especially if he was not sick. I was constantly watching over the two of them to ensure that they were looking after their mental health. By no means did I think we were over what had happened in December 2020, even though we were going through life almost as normal.

After some convincing from both Nathan and me, Trevor agreed to go to the party. Nathan was happy to have the house to himself for the first time since Marley passed. Whilst I had some misgivings about leaving him by himself overnight, he was keen to see the back of us and could not wait for us to drive off. Some of my concerns were, what if he found it hard to be on his own in the house by himself? What if he became lonely and sad? I sometimes forget that he is an adult. As a mum, you tend to worry about everything. I am sure I am not the only one.

The party was lovely. We were joined by two other lovely couples, one who we knew and the other we got to know during the course of the evening. Whilst I enjoyed myself, thoughts of Marley were not far off.

As I remembered just four years ago when I was celebrating a significant birthday with family and friends with no inkling that three years later, I would be heartbroken with the loss of Marley. Although Trevor had been reluctant to go, he enjoyed himself and did not take up the offer to retire to the hotel room if it got too much for him. He stayed and partied until the music was turned off at midnight. Over the years I have learnt that if there is an option to stay overnight in the hotel it is easier to convince him to go to an event. Knowing that there is a room within an arm's length that he could retire to if things got too much for him, takes away whatever reservations he might have had of attending the event. Nathan also had a good night. He had invited a few of his friends over for drinks so he had company.

Not long after, we received another invitation to my cousin's fiftieth birthday in Kent. It was also being held at a hotel with the option of staying overnight. On this occasion I could not convince Trevor to go with me. The fact that it was in November and most days were similar to 11 December did not help. I was a bit concerned that he would be on his own as around this time Nathan was working weekends and also late hours. On the morning when I was leaving, Trevor said, "I am going to be on my own when Nathan goes to work later." He is not one to make a fuss, but I read between the lines, the words which he had left unsaid. It was the first time that he would be on his own for that length of time and he would be lonely. It's not easy trying to second guess what was going through his mind but on this occasion, it was very clear. After he dropped me off at the train station, I texted two of his friends to pop round and see him as he would be on his own during the day. Fortunately, one of them could make it even though it was short notice. Trevor, like most men find it difficult to reach out for help even when they need it. I really thank God for friends who can be there for us at the drop of a hat. Similar to the other birthday celebrations, I realised that as much as I could enjoy myself to a certain extent, Marley and the similarity to my celebrations brought back memories. Still, it was good to get out there as I reconnected with family from America who I had not seen since the event of December 2020. I was able to talk about that day without tears which was a successful milestone in itself.

Before the pandemic, I used to do business travels two to three times a month. Since February 2020, I had not travelled and in October 2021, I had to travel to Sweden for business. It would be the first time I had travelled outside of the UK and stayed away from home since Marley had passed. I was not looking forward to it because I did not know how I would feel but until you try something you will never know. As we took steps forward in living without Marley, there would be things we would have to do, even if our natural instincts were to avoid it. I focused on the positive aspects of my travel: I would be seeing, and meeting team members based in Stockholm, Sweden, for the first time in real life as they had joined the team during lockdown. I had only met them on video calls. I was not travelling alone as I had a friend and colleague who was also based in the UK, and we would be travelling together so I had someone to keep me distracted.

When I look back at my trip, I am glad I did it as the other opportunity for travel would have been in December and I really did not want to travel at that time. The trip was successful, and I realised I could do it. There were moments when I felt sad, for example, when I met my previous manager who had been so supportive to me when Marley had passed, and also meeting other friends and colleagues for the first time since December. It was emotional, however, good to get that first meeting out of the way. Even though they were not there, I could tell that they shared some of the pain and loss I had experienced and was still experiencing. I had also used the opportunity to take the vests we would wear for Marley's 8KM Memory Walk with me.

8

Emotional Triggers—Mum's View

In the early days, one of the things we feared as a family was coming across people who had no clue that Marley was no longer with us. We had tried as best as we could to inform everyone who was close to us and those who were not so close. I had gone through my contacts to ensure that most people who knew him and us had been informed. Whilst going through my contacts I realised that there were still some friends whom I had missed because we had not been in contact with in the last two years or so. These people would have no idea. I was in two minds whether to reach out to them or not as I thought if there had not been any contact for that length of time, then it was likely that that would continue. So, I was a bit hesitant. I was forced to act when Trevor had an incident with someone who used to be close to us whilst the children were growing up.

Trevor had gone to our local shop and whilst he was there, he came across the mother of one of Nathan and Marley's childhood friend who we have had no contact with for over fifteen years. Trevor was not planning to say hello as he thought she would not recognise him. But even when you do not see someone for a long time – whether or not there have been physical changes – you still recognise one another. We think we can get away with not making eye contact. In most cases if we can identify the person, of course they will recognise us too. In this instance Trevor thought he could avoid eye contact and not have to make small talk. How wrong he was. He was soon accosted by this woman, with the question we have now come to dread, "How are the boys? They must be quite grown men now," she continued without noticing that Trevor had not yet responded to the first question or the tension this question had created.

After what felt like a long time but only a few minutes in reality, she noticed that Trevor had not said anything. So, she went on to say, "You are Nathan and Marley's dad, right?"

Trevor answered, "Yes, I am, although Marley is no longer with us." Trevor's response was not what she was expecting, and she became very emotional in the shop, which put Trevor in an uncomfortable position. I don't know about other people but when I am going through a painful situation and I am trying to be strong and I see someone else being emotional because of something that has happened to me it creates a trigger, it takes me back to that pain and loss. The woman was in tears and very visibly upset. It's not the answer you expect when you ask someone how their children are doing. The worst still was yet to come, the next dreaded question was "what did he die of"? Or how did he die? For the person asking the question, it is normal that you follow up with what took that person's life, usually sickness or an accident that the person had no control over. It is a tough question for the receiver as it triggers the pain and loss. I never knew how difficult those questions were until I was the receiver and, in a situation where I didn't want to answer. Trevor told her that Marley had ended his life and because she could not control her emotions, she was now attracting the attention of other shoppers. Trevor quickly said his goodbyes whilst she was still enquiring about me and promising to visit. It was difficult for Trevor. He did not want to share about Marley, and he was neither prepared to be asked those questions nor the impact his answers would have on the receiver. This incident definitely put us on our guard.

Due to the pandemic and lockdown, I had not been to the church building for service for a long time and though I joined the online church events, I had a choice of using video or just audio. My first time back to the church building was going to be emotional so I asked Nathan and Trevor to go with me. Nathan agreed but Trevor thought it would be too emotional for him. I decided to do this the Sunday before my birthday. I prayed that everyone I would meet had already knew that Marley passed so that I would not have to deal with questions which could trigger me emotionally. Although it was a beautiful service, I was very emotional for other reasons. This was the church where Marley was dedicated to God as a baby, attended Sunday school, and was a regular at the front as one of the children from Sunday school singing or part of a presentation. He was also Joseph in the nativity over the years, and it was the same church where we had held the farewell service for him ten months ago. It was bound to be emotional. The good thing was, Nathan was with me, and I got a lot of comfort from that. Whilst it was tough, I did not let it put me off going to the physical building as I thought the more, I went, the less painful it would be and this would become part of the new normal.

I purposed in my heart to go to Sunday service in the physical church once every month until I felt more comfortable and could go more often. I have read of other people finding it hard to go to church after losing someone, so I knew I was not alone in my feelings. It's not all cases it's because they are angry with God but because you meet people who forces you to face your loss head on because of something they say or do without knowing how emotionally fragile you are, even though it might be years after your loss. I must say that there has been only one occasion when someone has asked about Marley since I started going back to church. "How are the boys doing?" she had asked. On this occasion I decided not to go into details and just said that the boys were fine. She had wanted to continue on that topic, but I was very quick to change the focus from me to hers. Technically, I believe Marley is doing great where he is now. What I omitted to say is that he is no longer in his physical body but his spirit lives on.

Don't get me wrong, not everyone would get the memo of what happened that the family of four is now a family of three or that the person who is no longer with us left under traumatic circumstances. What is needed in these situations is some sensitivity. I suggest letting the person volunteer the information. Don't fire one question after the other to them.

There are other triggers which we would not be able to control. I had created a family WhatsApp group some years ago when I was travelling a lot and needed to send just one message to everyone instead of sending three. When Marley passed it was a silent agreement that we would not take him off the group, and we would keep the same profile picture of the four of us. You can imagine my surprise when ten months later I saw on my phone on the group chat, "Marley left". I was shocked. I thought Trevor or Nathan had taken him off the group. They had both got similar messages and were wondering if I had taken him off the group chat. We realised that none of us had done so and it must have been initiated by the owners of WhatsApp. It made me emotional as I was not expecting it and it also brought afresh the fact that he had left us, another unwanted reminder.

There was also the incident with the death certificate. I had delegated the task of getting the death certificate to Trevor as the interim certificate had caused me a lot of emotional stress. He had contacted the registry for births and deaths and paid the required fee. Three weeks later, what we thought was the certificate arrived, it took Trevor a few minutes to open the envelope as he knew what the contents were. After psyching himself to open it, it turned out that it was not ours. The registration office had sent us three certificates belonging to someone else. It was difficult for him to do it the first time and he had to do it again. Due to this error, he had to call them again and also to post the ones which another family was expecting but not received because they had had been sent to us, the wrong address. It seemed like something small, but these small things cause a lot of unwanted stress. On the second attempt the registration office got it right. When we got it out of the envelope, and you could see in black and white that Marley was gone, the impact on us was tough.

One of the things that really causes a trigger for me is the dates, which immediately bring Marley to the forefront of my mind. I am always thinking of what was happening around that time, not having the knowledge that the time with Marley was coming to an end. You hear people say what they would do if they knew their time on earth was coming to an end, but in this situation, I wonder what I would have done differently. Thinking about it but not wanting to dwell on it as that was the first advice we were given on that fateful day, there are definitely some things I would have done more of and some things I would have done less of. I would have listened more, spent more time with Marley than the "me time" I craved after a busy day at work. I would not have focused on the little things like leaving the water bottle empty in the fridge or taking the last tissue from the tissue box and leaving the empty box for someone else to put in the bin. I would definitely not have insisted that he spent his birthday money on the clothes that he did not live to enjoy.

In September 2021 Emma Raducanu, the British tennis player was making headlines in the news after becoming Britain's first female Grand Slam champion since 1977 for winning the US Open. I remember waking up that morning after she had won the final and being very happy for her and her parents, but then becoming very low in my spirit when it dawned on me that she was born the same year as Marley, less than a month before Marley was born. At the time she won the US Open she was eighteen, the same age as Marley was. I started thinking of all the stuff Marley could have achieved and what I had missed out on. Honestly, I could not understand why I was in pieces, crying my eyes out of what could have been, but there I was, reliving all the stuff that I thought I had cried out of my system. I must have cried for over thirty minutes before I felt better. Fortunately, I was alone downstairs so neither Nathan nor Trevor could hear me. After this incident I learnt that I could never prepare myself for every situation or event which could trigger off feelings of emotion. I had to depend on God. He is the one who gives me strength to face life head on.

With Nathan it's usually when he hears that someone else ended their life, especially when there is a sibling involved who has had to experience similar emotions to what he has gone through. This usually happens when he watches the news or social media. There was an occasion when he felt really sad because he was thinking that he would be on his own when Trevor and I passed. I listed all his numerous cousins in England, Sierra Leone and other countries. I assured him that he would be fine, especially if he goes on to have his own family. He has some really good friends who have continued to support him. The Bible says, "The man of too many friends [chosen indiscriminately] would be broken in pieces and come to ruin, but there is a [true, loving] friend who [is reliable and] sticks closer than a brother comes to mind" (Proverbs 18:24 AMP).

9

Overcoming Fear—Mum's View

The finality of death and the unknown is scary for all of us. When you die, how you die are some of the things that concern us. For some of us we are fearful of leaving others behind, even though we would not be around, the caretaker in us would worry about how the people we would leave behind would cope without us. For others they are fearful of losing the ones who are close to them as they could not imagine life without those people who they are close to. When someone dies in the family, this fear becomes even more real, especially when it was not expected. On the other hand, when someone is sick and the doctors give you a prognosis, if the prognosis is not good, even though you don't want to lose that person, you know that eventually they will pass and leave you and so you are forced to begin the grieving process whilst the loved one is still alive.

This was what I experienced when I lost my mum but that is a story for another day. Losing Marley in the way that we did caused me to be fearful of losing anyone else. It was all about the unexpected, not being in control of the future. It creates a fear that has no factual grounds apart from what has happened, the possibility that it could happen again gets a hold of you and becomes this fear that you cannot shake off. I know that this fear was not from God, but I had been hit hard by the unexpected. I was thinking we were now a family of three and if anything happens to any of us our family could be halved. You can imagine how I felt when Nathan suddenly started getting vertigo out of nowhere. The first episode was in February after Marley passed in December. He was so sick; he could not eat anything without throwing up. He had to be horizontal or he felt that everything was spinning around him. It was very worrying. He could only get telephone appointments with the doctor due to the pandemic and each medication prescribed was not effective. He started doing his own research on the internet and discovered some exercises which could help. After three to four days, he felt better. I had reached everyone who could pray to lift him up in prayer. When he got better, we thought that was the end of it. But it wasn't. A few months later in May, he was confined to his bed again with the same thing. The difference this time was that he knew it was coming as he started feeling the same way he had felt the last time before he was sick and confined to his bed.

A few days later he got better only for him to be sick again. We could not understand what was causing it. The doctors at the surgery could not see him physically and were making a diagnosis based on phone appointments, which was frustrating and unhelpful. He had started looking for employment but because of being handicapped by the vertigo it made him reluctant to get a job. How could he start working and then take time off for sickness? When he felt better, I booked the three of us for a private health check. I wanted to get to the bottom of this.

In September we had the health check and the results came back three weeks later. We were all fine, nothing was wrong, however, mid-October he had another episode. We were slowly accepting that this was something that he may have to live with but in my heart, I was not accepting it. When he recovered, I encouraged him to look for the jobs that he had been interested in and for him to apply as not working was causing him to be down. He succeeded and in November he started working again. He had only been working for a week when he came home rushing to the bathroom because he was sick. I thought enough is enough. When he got into his bed, I said I was going to pray for him. I had prayed before but nothing like this. I was angry, very angry and I thought to myself, I have to put a stop to this so help me God. I told him we were not going to accept vertigo popping on and off and stopping him from living a normal life. I remember putting my hands on his head and prayed, commanding the vertigo and everything associated with it to go in Jesus' name. I also asked for wisdom and knowledge to know what the root cause was for the vertigo so that Nathan could address it. Afterwards I said to him, "You need to stop eating tuna." In October he had a lot of tuna and pasta. It was his favourite comfort food. I told him not to eat any more of it for the rest of the year.

He looked at me and said, "How could you just pray like that?"

"What do you mean?" I asked. It was not the first time he had heard me praying so I was curious to hear what his reply was.

"The words just flow from you, without you mumbling or thinking. It seems so natural," he responded.

"It's the Holy Spirit in me," I said. "You need to trust God now for your healing and stop eating tuna."

He just smiled and said, "We will see."

As I write, it's been ten months since he had that episode in November. He actually admitted that he has never felt better. He has not eaten tuna and he is feeling great. That incident caused me to trust God even more for my family. I hold on to what The Bible says, "No temptation has overtaken you except what is common to mankind. And God is faithful; he would not let you be tempted beyond what you could bear" (1 Corinthians 10:13 AMP). I have to trust God; he cares for me and if anything happens, he allowed it for a reason. I am constantly talking to him about Marley and asking if there could be another way, but each time it's almost as if it's an audible voice saying to me, "it was the only option that I would be able to bear". I don't think I am special or closer to God than the next person, but I slowly started to believe that we are all on this earth for a purpose and we will be here for as long as we have been purposed.

In our human thinking we put time into two boxes; a longer period of time and a shorter period of time, but God is timeless and we might say that Marley had a short life, but he had served his purpose. I am still here because there is more God has purposed for me to do and you are still here because there is still a purpose you need to achieve. When I focus on this thinking it really helps me to overcome the fear of losing someone. If God could not hold back His Son, Jesus, then who am I to question God on the timing of when Marley left us. This is not to say that it does not sometimes cloud my Godly thinking especially when I feel the loss and pain of losing someone. I have to ask myself, why would I become fearful of losing someone else in the family? God is in control and we are all here for a purpose.

10

A Beautiful Day—Mum's View

The first anniversary of Marley's passing was fast approaching and as a family there were different emotions we were experiencing as December approached. First and foremost was the first birthday without him and what that would look like. I had decided earlier on that there would not be a memorial service as the focus in December would not be on his passing. I was more focused on the day he had been born to us, which would always be special. It made sense that the first official event to raise funds collectively as trustees would be a memory walk on the Saturday closest to his birth date, Saturday 4 December 2021. The Saturday after what would have been Marley's nineteenth birthday, we had the first Marley's 8KM Memory Walk to raise funds for Marley's Aart Foundation.

A lot of planning had gone into making this day special. Time had been spent choosing the route for the walk. It needed to be the route which Marley had frequented, therefore the route leading to his secondary school, the bike shop Decathlon and his first school where he had such happy memories were also included. Once it was clear what landmarks needed to be included, it was important that we did a test walk to get an idea of how long it would take and that the walk would be about five miles, which is just over eight kilometres. On the day I did this with one of the trustees, it was a clear day. Trevor dropped us off at the starting point which was Marley's secondary school, and we walked through the town centre going past most of the places which he used to frequent including part of the route he used to do for his paper round with the end point being his first school.

I had contacted both schools to inform them of our intentions to use one or the other as our starting and end point. I did not expect that both schools would want to play some part in it. The secondary school wanted a few of the teachers to join and the primary school wanted to serve us refreshments at the end of the walk. I was really touched. I had a meeting with the head teacher of St Christopher's Academy before the walk. I took Nathan with me and as we walked, we relived some of the childhood memories when I would drop them off at school (which did not happen very often as they had their auntie who was staying with us at the time to take them to school). As we were walking, I looked ahead of me and noticed a boy who looked exactly like a young Marley wearing the St Christopher's uniform approaching us. It was like being taken back in time to all those years ago when Marley attended the school. I looked at Nathan thinking I was probably looking for Marley in every boy with some similarity but then Nathan looked at me and said, "Do you see what I see?"

"Are you looking at the young boy walking towards us?" I said.

"Yes, I am," he said.

We both agreed he looked so much like a younger Marley. I was shocked that he had seen the same resemblance that I had seen. It was almost like a sign that we were doing the right thing. When the boy got closer, we could clearly see the resemblance, but not a strong lookalike as it had appeared from afar.

It was an emotional moment when we arrived at the school, and though there were aesthetic changes on the outside, the reception was much the same as when Nathan and Marley had attended. We were introduced to the head teacher who we had never met before but soon realised we had kindred spirit. It was uncanny how she had gone through incidents recently which I could relate to. She had also spoken to a few teachers who remembered Marley and Nathan when they attended the school and they had dug up some photos of Marley which we did not have. It was a very touching visit and it also confirmed that we were making the right decision to end the walk at Marley's first school. We also accepted the hospitality being offered by the head teacher.

Towards the end of November, beginning of December, Covid cases were rising across the country, and I was happy I had encouraged supporters to walk in their location. I did not want everyone to join us in the memory walk locally as it would have been too many people. There were people in other countries also who wanted to support me and the foundation, so I encouraged anyone who was not local to walk where they were and to take videos and pictures, they would share with me afterwards. We had successfully sourced a number of vests with the foundation's name and logo, which were adapted from Marley's YouTube channel's logo by a close friend who had spent time with Nathan and Marley at a young age.

On the morning of the walk, I woke up early. I was not sure how many people would join us as I had received a few messages the days leading up to the walk that they had caught Covid and therefore could not join in. There were other unforeseen circumstances which meant not all of the trustees could join the walk either. God is so faithful because whilst I was getting these negative signs, I also got this innate assurance that I was doing the right thing even though there were circumstances and events which made me question if indeed it was the right thing. I really believed that this was what God wanted me to do. Also, the weather forecast for the days leading up to the walk and the day itself was not brilliant and there was a likelihood that it would be a snowy day. I was thinking that it might end up being just Nathan and me walking. How wrong I was.

I went to bed the day before the walk with all these thoughts going through my mind but God has a way of confirming again and again that He is in control. First of all, the day before the walk which would have been Marley's birthday, the scripture from Psalm 118:24, "This [day in which God has saved me] is the day which the LORD has made; Let us rejoice and be glad in it." I have a pack of cards with different scripture verses which can be changed daily. When I changed the card the scripture which was next was this one which was what I had put in Marley's eighteenth birthday card the year before. For me it was not coincidental that this same scripture was on the card I had changed that morning. On his birthday when I could have been sad it felt as if God was saying to me, it's another day, which

He has made and just as I was saying to Marley to be happy about it, God was now saying the same thing to me. I also felt that all would be alright. I told Nathan and he did not know what to say; even though he could be sceptical about such things he realised that I was definitely getting comfort from God, as I could easily have been in tears because Marley was not with us to celebrate his birthday.

It was forecast to rain on the morning of the walk; however, I was determined that Nathan and I would still do the walk. There were some friends and family who were planning to meet us at home since I had asked Trevor to do a few drop-offs at the starting point. When Trevor dropped Nathan and me at the starting point, I was pleasantly surprised to see that about thirty to thirty-five people were already there waiting for us to start the walk. We distributed the colours to those who had not yet got the vest and we were ready to set off. As we walked the rain clouds disappeared and the sun was shining. The morning became a bright and sunny day even if it was still cold. There were people from our church as well as friends and family who joined us for the walk. I was leading the way as I was the only one who knew the exact route, since I had done the test walk.

Whilst we were walking, I was receiving text messages from supporters in different parts of the country who were also doing the five-mile walk. I was really touched when I received a picture of friends and colleagues in Stockholm, Sweden, who were also doing the walk in the snow-covered roads but with a bright shining sun. It was fantastic. In just over two hours we reached our end point, St Christopher's Academy. There was a sign at the gate welcoming Marley's Aart Foundation, which made me emotional.

When we got in, I was expecting teas and coffees not a spread of cakes and biscuits and lovely food which had been prepared and laid out for us. I was really touched by the kindness and generosity of the head teacher and the school. A heartfelt thank you to all who made it a beautiful day – the first Marley's 8KM Memory Walk.

11

CAN DECEMBER BE BEAUTIFUL AGAIN?—MUM'S VIEW

There is no doubt in our minds that the month of December would never be the same again after 2020, but how could we make it bearable, if not beautiful again? These are some of the questions which were going through our minds as we were counting down from November to December in 2021. I have already mentioned in Chapter Four – Marley's Legacy, about the foundation we set up and the first Marley's 8KM Memory Walk, which would take place every year, either Saturday before or after his birthday. There was another date, the 11 December, which was imprinted in our minds and the days after which we needed to navigate. I had hoped that the memorial headstone for the grave would be ready for installation but due to delays with raw materials, the masons at the funeral home could not get it ready in time. I had given a lot of thought to what we should do as the first anniversary of Marley's passing approached. I thought about having a memorial service or something but in the end, I wanted to keep it low key. I did not want anything that would trigger a lot of emotions of loss and grief. We were on a high from the walk which had generated support nationwide, across Europe and in Africa, and I was really happy with the support and donations from everyone which would enable Marley's Aart to make a difference in another young person's life.

The week leading to the eleventh I had a call with CHUMS, one of the organizations Marley's Aart was funding to provide Art Therapy for young people. In this call I was really encouraged that the first young person Marley's Aart was funding was a young boy aged nine and he had already had eight sessions with more to come. It was significant for me that within a year of such a traumatic loss, the pain of losing Marley was already turning into something positive. And also, because the first young person was a boy and younger made it even more significant. It is important to address any mental health issues in the very early stages as the older the young person gets, the more they are unwilling to accept help. I know this from the experience with Marley. If we had caught on at the very early stage when Marley had just transferred to his new school that he needed professional intervention, I strongly believe this would have made a difference. As around this time he was complaining about fitting in and not being able to make lasting friendships, we would have had a chance to make a difference as he would have been more receptive to it. I was feeling positive after the feedback from CHUMS regarding this young boy. It made facing the anniversary a bit more bearable.

My aunt from London had told me she would be coming to spend the day with us, being that the first anniversary would be on a Saturday. I had taken the Friday and the Monday off work as I did not want to be blindsided by the emotions that had overwhelmed me in June. We had plans to go to the cemetery to lay some flowers. My aunt was arriving earlier by train so she could go with us. I am always in a surreal state when I go to the cemetery. Part of me accepts that it is the reality, but the more time passes the more I feel like Marley went somewhere else. He seemed removed from the reality of what we experienced. It's almost as if it was somebody else. Maybe thinking like this helps me to cope with the reality, but this is how I feel when I visit his grave. I am always asking the question why? I am there but it is as if I am not there. Thoughts are constantly going through my head. Am I really here visiting Marley's grave? Is this real? It is hard to believe the reality.

When we got home from the cemetery, my aunt started preparing the usual traditional food of black-eyed beans with fried plantains and sweet potatoes, which could be eaten on their own or with white rice. Nathan had to go to work. I had encouraged him to take the time off, but he had assured me that he would be alright. Trevor was watching football whilst my aunt and I were preparing the food. I am glad that she was with us as whilst I had told friends and family that we were keeping it low key and did not want a fuss, it was good to have another female in our home. I had never navigated this road before so I did not know what I really needed. After we finished preparing the food, we were about to have dinner when a close friend stopped by. Unfortunately for her another friend of hers had lost her daughter unexpectedly and she had been on her way back home from visiting this friend. When I hear of another family, another mother going through the loss of their child, my heart bleeds for them. It is different now that I have experienced it compared to before when I had not had that experience.

Later, I dropped my aunt at the station as she returned to London. We had survived the first anniversary. What's next? Christmas was approaching but it did not feel like it. In previous years around the second weekend after Marley's birthday would be the time when we put up Christmas decorations both inside and outside our house. We were not in the mood, but I felt I had to shake off this feeling. We had to move forward to embracing some parts of December. Yes, it would never be the same but in my heart, I really believed that if Marley could have had a say in this, he would want us to at least put up the Christmas tree.

On Sunday 12 December, I decided that I would put up the Christmas tree. Trevor and Nathan were opposed to it, but I knew once I had the tree up, they would come round. Trevor got me all the stuff from the loft, and I put the tree up. I found it really helpful as the mood in our home changed. It no longer felt sad and empty. All around us, the neighbours had put up some form of Christmas decorations. When coming home in the evening our house – which used to be lit up around this time of the year – was the only one in a cluster of about five houses with no Christmas lights, no indication that Christmas was round the corner. I was not yet ready to put any Christmas lights outside and maybe I will never be ready for that as we had done in the past, but I felt this was a good step forward. I also got some lights for the windows at the front of the house which included Marley's room. Marley always loved to have lights in his room so I was glad I could do it this year. Last year we were in no position to do this but this year we could. I also put in the order for some of the other food stuff we usually have for Christmas.

After all the plans I had made for Christmas, on Christmas Eve I tested positive for Covid, so Christmas day was not the same. Nathan was trying to stay away from me but he could not prepare the meal we had planned. Trevor was resigned to the fact that he, too, probably had Covid so there was no point in him isolating himself from me. By Boxing Day, all of us had Covid. It was good that we had no plans to visit with family as it would have been a disaster. Since it was just the three of us, we made the best of it. I pushed for us to prepare the food we had planned as surprisingly we had not lost our appetite. After the holidays I thought it would be good if we could do something different together the following year.

God has a way of bringing some good in a dark day. Whilst December would no longer be the same, I was pleasantly surprised when on 31 December 2021, one of my nieces who was expecting her baby between Christmas and the New Year, gave birth to a baby boy. Indeed, God could make life beautiful again as The Bible says, "To grant to those who mourn in Zion the following: To give them a turban instead of mourning, The garment of praise instead of a disheartened spirit. So, they would be called the trees of righteousness [strong and magnificent, distinguished for integrity, justice and right standing with God], The planting of the Lord, that He may be glorified" (Isaiah 61:3 AMP).

Without any prior knowledge he was given two names of significance to Marley and our family. The first of which was Benjamin after Marley's granddad and the second was Trevor's middle name, Anthony. I really felt that God was saying something unique in the situation. First significance was the extended family had been blessed with another male child and second the names were very significant because of the connection to Marley. I was so happy for my niece and her husband as this was the niece who had got married in February 2021 on the same day as Nathan's birthday. I believed that God was turning our mourning into dancing as The Bible says, "You have turned my mourning into dancing for me; You have taken off my sackcloth and clothed me with joy, that my soul may sing praise to You and not be silent. O Lord my God, I will give thanks to You forever" (Psalm 30:11-12 AMP).

12

The Dark Clouds Will Get Lighter—Mum's View

If you have read my first book *Marley's Memoir: The Journey to an Irreversible Action and the Aftermath,* you would already know that I'm a Christian and have a very strong faith in God. Similar to the first book I have included bible references in some of the chapters, and also the gospel songs for those who would understand the context and would draw strength from them. I hope that there would be a lot of people from other faiths or religions who would read this book, and I would like to say I could only refer to what I know and what has really been a source of strength for me and my family during this difficult time. There are also others who have no faith or religion, and I hope you will also get something out of reading this book.

It is usual after a traumatic loss in a family that as the days become weeks, the weeks become months, and months become years, that those who were there for you in the first phase of loss move on with life and it seems as if everyone around you has accepted that this is how it is now. This period, which is the phase we are now in, could be difficult. Whilst you would not want everyone to be reminding you of the traumatic event of that day, on the other hand you don't want them to forget that someone significant to you is missing. It's also difficult for those around you who could be in the wrong if they keep bringing up reminders of that day, yet it could be insensitive if they barely acknowledge it. It is not because they have forgotten but because they don't want to keep reminding you of it. It is more difficult for the immediate family.

I have heard of marriages breaking up after traumatic events such as this. Couples spend time blaming each other for the event or expecting the other partner to grieve in the same way as the other is grieving. We have to accept that we are all different when it comes to a lot of things, especially grief. One person grieves differently to another. It is normal for women to be more expressive in their grief but if you are the husband and your wife is not being expressive in her grieving, don't hold it against her, be supportive in whatever form she copes with her grief. There are even cultural differences in the way we grieve. In my African culture there is a more visible expression of grief compared to the British culture. It's important that we understand this and support each other in the way we express our grief. I could not imagine being separated from Trevor at this time. We have shared so many memories with Marley. Whilst he may express himself in a different way to me and I have felt this strong call to do the things I have been doing to help others, it does not mean that he loved Marley less or he does not want his memory to live on. I have to understand that it is my calling not his. Who knows if God may call him to do something later on? My advice to couples who may be going through something similar is to keep the communication going with each other and encourage each other.

I would like to encourage any parents who have gone through similar traumatic events of losing a child to avoid blaming each other or looking back and thinking if one or the other had been more accommodating this situation would not have happened. If you love each other don't make it worse by putting guilt on each other as it makes it harder to deal with the difficult emotions and loss that you would be feeling. You may have experienced other types of grief, like losing your parents or sibling but losing your child, for me, is so much worse in my opinion and I know because I have lost both parents and some of my siblings.

It does get bearable, though. I don't say better because I am not there yet. The physical pain which used to engulf me every time I think about Marley is not as sharp as it was. I remember attending a bereavement seminar in 2021 and one of the leaders shared this visual with us. When you lose someone the pain of the loss was symbolised with a beach ball and a glass bowl symbolised the capacity of the person who is bereaved. In the first few months, the image showed that the ball could not fit in the bowl because the person does not have the capacity to comprehend what happened. As time goes by the ball remains the same size but the capacity to comprehend what happened gets bigger. The image showed the size of the bowl gets bigger whilst the size of the ball remains the same, and over time it could fit completely in the bowl, not because the ball gets smaller but because the bowl gets bigger. There are books on loss and grief which could guide us; reading the testimonies of other people and experiencing the reality could be two completely different things. We have to trust God if we believe in Him, and if we don't, we must trust our instincts that we're doing the right things for all concerned, spouses, children and other affected parties. I do encourage all to trust in God because He has been such a tower of strength for me during these dark days. Proverbs 18: 10 The name of the LORD is a strong tower; The righteous runs to it and is safe and set on high [far above evil].

I want to iterate that mental health issues come in different forms; from what I have learnt in this short period of time since I lost Marley and continue to learn is that it is very important to seek early intervention if you are not sure. Get outside help, get professional expertise to make sense of what you or your loved one are experiencing. Parents do all you can to get younger children showing similar symptoms diagnosed to rule out any early stages of mental-health issues, since they are more receptive to intervention at an early age. There are lots of organizations out there who can support you.

Finally, I hope our story helps you cope with whatever difficult situation you are facing and draw strength and hope from our experience; indeed the dark clouds will get lighter and you will smile again.

Epilogue

Since the events covered in this book, a lot has happened. The foundation which I founded in May 2021 has now been registered as a charity in England and Wales. Prior to the registration Marley's Aart funded individual art therapy for a young boy between the ages of eight and ten. This was made possible because of the child trust fund which Marley never got to spend and the donations to the fundraising events, 7KG @7mths by Rosemary Peck and Marley's 8KM Memory Walk. Following the registration Marley's Aart has also funded group art therapy for six young people with mental health issues. We have also funded a workshop for parents and their children who are having anxiety and other mental health issues.

The foundation is making a difference funding art therapy for young people with mental health issues not only through CHUMS but more recently in schools. Starting with Marley's previous secondary school the foundation now funds individual and group art therapy for the students who have been suffering with anxiety and social disorder as well as transition and settling issues from primary to secondary school.

The second Marley's 8KM Memory Walk in December 2022 was well attended with 10% more people joining the local walk compared to the previous year. The number of locations where friends, family and supporters walked also increased compared to the previous year. When I started the foundation and planned the memory walk to coincide with Marley's birthdate, it was meant to be primarily a day for us to remember Marley publicly and to raise funds for his legacy. I did not foresee that the walk would raise awareness for others to check their mental health and be more open to talking to others about it. After the second walk I received feedback from people from different locations sharing how the walk created an opportunity for people to connect and talk about their feelings and who they could reach out to for help.

Acknowledgments

I am grateful to the support I have received from family, friends, my church Luton Christian Fellowship and the BSBS (Bedfordshire Suicide Bereavement Services) during these difficult months. Without the support of my husband Trevor and my son Nathan, I would not have written this second book. Above all I want to thank God for strengthening me and giving me a purpose, turning my pain to a purpose.

Organizations That Can Help

You can support the work Marley's Aart Foundation is funding by making donations on the website: www.marleysaartfoundation.com

Worldwide Organizations you could reach out to if you are concerned about the mental health of a loved one or you need to speak to someone:

CALM – Campaign Against Living Miserably

https://www.thecalmzone.net/international-mental-health-charities

CBM – Christian Blind Mission

https://www.cbmuk.org.uk/what-we-do/mental-health/

Choosing Therapy

https://www.choosingtherapy.com/top-mental-health-organizations/

MIND

https://www.mind.org.uk

HE CARES

You Are Not Alone When Navigating Loss

MAJENDI JARRETT

FOREWORD BY
ALAN WEST

HE CARES

YOU ARE NOT ALONE WHEN NAVIGATING LOSS

I would like to dedicate this book to all close family members I have lost. And to all who have lost close family members, I would like to say that God cares—you are never alone.

Contents

Foreword by Alan West...235

Acknowledgments...237

Introduction...239

1 Mum Is Coming...241

2 Gone Too Soon, or Was It?...248

3 Standing on the Word...255

4 An Offer I Could Not Resist...262

5 Embracing My New Surroundings...267

6 Settling in My New Life...272

7 Settled but Unsettled...281

8 Surprises and Challenges...288

9 First and Last Christmas...294

10 Saying Goodbye to Mum...300

11 Planning Mum's Service...307

12 Different Losses: How Do They Compare?...314

13 Marley, Always in My Heart...319

14 Final Words...326

15 Epilogue: Three Years & Nine Months Later...333

Foreword

This book approaches a subject we all would like to shy away from. No one wants to face the painful reality of grief, bereavement, and death. But the way Majendi Jarrett writes and speaks through these pages about her personal experiences of grief and bereavement are so real, and her honesty, truthfulness, and candid approach are so inspiring and humbling, that she gives hope to all of us who will one day also face the loss of someone we love.

I've personally known Majendi and her family for twenty-five years or so. I've been their pastor and friend during that time. Again, she speaks openly and candidly about her faith in God and her personal walk with Christ, which has given her the strength, faith, and courage to carry on and face tomorrow. Jesus has been her closest friend in her time of need. I've personally seen from close range how she has coped in recent years after the tragic death of her son Marley. Her faith has been a rock on which she has stood and has given hope to so many. It was Jesus Himself who taught us to build our lives on something rock solid, not on the shifting sands of this fragile world's standards, so that when the storms of life hit us, we will miraculously survive, as we are anchored to eternal truth.

I'm a father of two sons and the thought of losing one of them is too painful to contemplate. Majendi has helped me, and I know her story will help and encourage many who will face in their life's journey the reality and pain of grief and bereavement with HOPE and COURAGE.

Alan West
Retired pastor of Luton Christian Fellowship and former football player at Burnley, Luton Town, and Millwall (UK) and of the Minnesota Kicks (USA)

Acknowledgments

Above all I want to thank God for strengthening me and giving me a purpose, turning my pain to a purpose. He has given me the strength and the boldness to write this book and my other two books.

Without the support of my husband Trevor and my son Nathan, I would not have written any of the books, much more this one. Thank you, Trevor and Nathan, for your continuous love and support.

I also want to acknowledge Pastor Mike Nicholls who gave me the inspiration for the title of this book and Alan West for being so kind to write the foreword for this book.

I am grateful for the support I have received from family, friends, my church (Luton Christian Fellowship), and the BSBS (Bedfordshire Suicide Bereavement Services) during these difficult months.

I also want to thank some special people who have been constantly asking me when the third book will be released. These people do not how much they have encouraged me by just asking about it. There was a time before I started writing the third book that I thought I would only have two books in the Loss and Grief series, but then I was reminded that I had said that there will be two books after I launched my first.

Introduction

In this book I want to share about the grief and loss journeys I went through before losing my son Marley. Whilst there are similarities, there are significant differences between death by sickness and death by suicide.

I want to give insight into the circumstances and the time frame of these previous losses, how old I was both physically (since I was born) and spiritually (since I became a believer), and most importantly how God has always been there for me, even at times when it did not feel like it.

I also want to show how the closeness I shared with each person described in this book impacted me in different ways.

I want also to tell everyone who reads this book that there is hope. A transition takes place when we go through losses; we are birthed into something new. This could be a new direction, a new country, or something else.

I hope that everyone who has lost someone will be able to relate to the feelings and circumstances I share in this book.

1

Mum Is Coming

No one can escape the pain of losing someone. Sooner or later, we will all go through it. Depending on your character, losing someone you love and care for might be the hardest thing you will ever have to face, the hardest thing you will ever have to go through. When you experience it for the first time, it can be really tough. Loss can almost paralyse you, depending on how close you were to the person who passed.

My first experience of deep loss was my brother, Frank Dinsdale Bowen Wright. I lost him at the young age of twenty-nine. It was the first time I lost someone who I was not expecting to die. It was the first time I lost someone who was young. It was the first time I lost someone who was very close to me, and it was the first time that my faith as a believer was tested.

Though I had lost other family members before losing my brother, those losses did not hit me as hard. Perhaps it was because the people were not so close to me—an elderly aunt or uncle, other distant relations, or a friend's mother. However, even when I lost my dad, it was not as difficult as when I lost my brother. I think because I had never lived in the same house as my dad, I did not have the kind of really close, loving relationship with him that I did with my brother.

Frank and I grew up together. He was four years older than me, so in our teens we experienced all the same growing pains of being punished or told off by our mum because we were out late or because we did not do our chores. He was protective of me when we were out partying and young boys were trying to chat me up. We shared our teenage years together.

I have vivid memories of our home in Congo Cross, Banana Water. I remember us playing outside during the school holidays, then rushing to get indoors as soon as we spotted our mum coming home from work. I would usually be much closer to the house than Frank and my other brother Raymond because they would be doing the forbidden: playing football in the street. They were not allowed to do this, as it was not a football field and they could easily have gotten hit by a car. We used to live in the second floor of a two-storey house, so I would be downstairs, playing catchers or skipping with the neighbour's children who were closer to my age. Then suddenly I would see Frank sprinting towards me, racing up the stairs shouting, "Mum is coming!" Just thinking about it now brings a smile to my face. At 16 he was all long legs in his shorts, dashing towards the house, closely followed by Raymond. This would be my cue either to run upstairs and sit quietly with a book or to race to complete any chores that were left undone whilst we were playing with our neighbours.

If we were successful, Mum would not have a clue that we had been playing outside, and if she was in a good mood, she would even turn a blind eye to the fact that we were only just doing our chores then, when we had

had the whole rest of the day to do them. We would be grinning at each other behind her back, knowing we had narrowly escaped being told off for doing exactly what she had told us not to do.

It's not that she did not want us to play outside. But there were several reasons why she discouraged us from doing so. First, she was a very quiet and introverted person and she knew that our playing outside could have led to issues with other children or neighbours, which could have created tension. Neighbours were always falling out because of their children. There was also the chance that we would mistakenly kick the football against a glass window or hit an older person with it, either of which would have meant unnecessary expenses that our mum could not afford. Also, if someone *had* gotten hit—especially an older person—they would have brought a complaint against us. As children, we did not understand these reasons. We were more concerned with our enjoyment. Fortunately, we never broke any windows or hit anyone with the ball.

On other occasions when we were not quick enough and she saw my brothers on the street playing football, we would get an earful from her. She would go on all evening until we went to bed. At the time I thought she was a party pooper, stopping us from having fun, but as I got older, I saw things a bit more from her perspective. She wanted us to be safe. Sometimes the cars were being driven too fast, and a few children had been hit by a car and ended up with a broken leg or arm, and she did not want that for us. As children we did not understand this.

I also have memories of Frank and Raymond hitting puberty and becoming very conscious of their body image. As we all grew up, we lost whatever puppy fat we had and became mostly long arms and legs. I can recall Frank and Raymond discovering that press-ups would build their muscles and competing with each other to see who could do the most. Of course, being the only girl, I did not want to be left out of the fun, so I would also join them in doing the press-ups. Though of course I would be the first to give up because my arms were aching and I could not do anymore. Frank was very competitive and, being the eldest of the three of us, he wanted to be the one that did the most press-ups. Afterwards he would flex his muscles and show off to Raymond that he was stronger. The more press-ups they did, the more toned and more conscious of their body image they became, especially when they started attracting the attention of girls. I enjoyed a few freebies from girls who Frank dated or who wanted to be noticed by him. It was typical in those days for girls to be nice to us younger siblings so we would put in a good word for her to my brother.

I especially remember one girl who I got quite close with. She was older than me and she used to do my hair very nicely. She was very particular in the way she dressed and presented herself, and she had met Frank because they were both part of a local choir close to where we lived. I really liked her, and every time I would go to her to do my hair, I would be there a long time. So, my mum started getting very concerned. She was not happy that I had a friend who was older than me. She thought the girl would be a bad influence on me. What she did not know at the time was that I was the messenger for Frank. There were no mobile phones in those days, and we did not even have a landline at home. So, when I went by her to do my hair, I would pass messages to her from Frank, and she would give me a message for him in return. Usually, he was letting her know that he would be at choir practice so they could see each other.

Unfortunately, their relationship did not last very long because she became very jealous and possessive over Frank. He attracted a lot of girls because of his musical talent. (His dad had been a talented musician, so I believe he inherited his talents from him.) Even though he was not interested in these other girls, she was not happy with his having any of these friendships with them, so they split up. She and I continued to be friends until Mum put a stop to it and told me that I had to get someone else closer to my age to do my hair.

As I said, Frank was a very talented musician. He could play the organ, piano, clarinet, and trombone, to name a few of the many instruments he had played. He was part of a few choirs and bands because of his talent. I used to enjoy watching and listening to him play the clarinet at home, as this was one of the instruments he could take with him after practice, whilst I could only see and hear him play the organ when we went to church as we did not have a piano at home. He had very long and slender fingers and they would race across the keyboard as if it was magic, and you would hear all these beautiful notes. I always thought that he was going to be famous and travel the world because of his musical talent.

Whilst we had a lot of good times, it would not be a normal childhood if we did not have our sibling squabbles. Like any normal family, we had our ups and downs. We did fall out a few times. Usually, it was over food, as food was always scarce when we were young. As teenagers, my brothers had big appetites. We were always fighting over food. Either one person's portion was too big or they had eaten someone else's share. Also, Frank, being the eldest son of the three of us, was very big on respect, and he would not tolerate Raymond or I being disrespectful to him. Kissing our teeth at him—a very common way to disrespect someone in the African community—would get him very angry. Also, when food was scarce, if we ate anything of his, this would not go down well. It would be a time of testing out the muscles Frank and Raymond had developed from the press-ups. Sometimes I would try to intervene between the two of them and would be at the receiving end of some punches in the crossfire. It definitely made me wiser, though, and gave me a better understanding of how to throw punches.

I will never forget one Christmas Eve when Frank and Raymond had decided to go out clubbing. Mum had told them they had to be back before midnight. Since they did not have keys to the house, they had to be back before she locked the door for the night. At that time, I was still too young to be allowed to go out with them; they must have been seventeen and nineteen and I was only fifteen. They stayed out beyond their curfew and Mum locked the door so that they could not get in. They threw some rocks at the window to get my attention so I could open the door and let them in, but Mum had hidden the key. They stayed outside until about 2 am before she finally let them in. Then they had to endure a telling-off that would go on for hours. It did not matter that it was so early in the morning. Later we had to go to our aunt's home for Christmas dinner, so the telling-off would go up another level, as they would now be told off by our aunts and our grandmother and any other older relative who had been invited to the holiday meal.

I always felt protected by my brothers, though, especially by Raymond as we went to the same primary school. He used to fight anyone who wanted to take advantage of me. When I was old enough to go out at night, I always had either Frank or Raymond with me. I was never on my own, and I loved it. It was great to have two brothers close to my age, though it also had its disadvantages, as most of the boys who were attracted to me were not brave enough to approach me because of my brothers. But I did not mind, because I thought if a boy really cared, he would be man enough to not be put off by my brothers.

2

Gone Too Soon, or Was It?

I became a believer in and follower of our Lord Jesus Christ when I was in my second year at university in Sierra Leone. I had heard messages about salvation a number of times, but a series of events that happened around this time caused everything to finally click.

I had always been concerned about being one of those believers who accepted Jesus as their personal saviour but then did not show any fruits or character worthy of the Lord. This was one of the reasons why it took me so long; I used to look at other believers and the way they acted and I would be the judge and jury, condemning them for not living the life of a believer. Even though I was not a believer, I would judge them on what I thought a believer should or should not do. This was something that God had to deal with me on personally to ensure that I took the step of faith. It was my own personal relationship with God and nobody else's that Jesus was concerned about. I cannot say it was because of this person or that person that I had not received my salvation for which Jesus had paid the price. It was also not guaranteed that, by putting it off, I would be ready, that I would not run out of time. As tomorrow is not promised to us, we have today and we have now. We need to open our hearts and not keep saying *I will do it tomorrow* or *next week* or *next year, after I have done this, that, or the other.* The Bible says,

> "Do not harden your hearts as [your fathers did] in the rebellion [of Israel at Meribah], On the day of testing in the wilderness."
>
> (Hebrews 3:8)

I was definitely hardening my heart against taking the step of faith prior to my second year at university. Once I received the revelation that I was trying to do things in my own strength and not leaning on God, I felt better. I realised that I can only do this through Christ who strengthens me, as it says in these verses:

> "I can do all things [which He has called me to do] through Him who strengthens *and* empowers me [to fulfill His purpose—I am self-sufficient in Christ's sufficiency; I am ready for anything and equal to anything through Him who infuses me with inner strength and confident peace]."
>
> (Philippians 4:13)

Once I said the sinner's prayer, I was committed. I hungered and thirsted for the things of God. I attended a Saturday Bible school that was next door to where I lived. I learnt a lot and fed my spirit with the word of God, which enabled my faith to grow very strong.

I looked forward to the weekends: I would get home from university on Friday then I would spend Saturday at Bible school and Sunday in church. I was committed. I could not get enough of the word of God, the preaching, the praise and worship. I also started attending an all-night prayer meeting on Friday nights with a few friends, and I was seeing the word of God coming to life at those events. Being a new believer, I did not think there was anything I could ask God for, according to His word, that I would not receive. Don't get me wrong—I still believe that now, but I have more context than I did then. I know that God's will and purpose for me also plays a very important part in what I receive when I ask. I was raw and new and on fire, and I wanted everyone who could listen to hear what Jesus did for us and how He changed my life.

Before my final year at university, I experienced a big change in my life. My mum moved to England because my stepdad was sick and dying of cancer. Since Frank had moved out when he got married and my other brother Raymond was living with our aunt, before my mum left for England, she made plans for me to live with some of our other relations whom I had grown close to in recent years.

Frank would always arrange transportation for me when I needed to go back to campus after summer vacation and this time was no different. I had reached out to him the weekend before my birthday both to arrange my transportation and to invite him to my birthday celebrations; I was planning to have a few close friends and family round for my birthday and

I was expecting that he, his wife, and their nine-month-old daughter would attend.

On that Saturday he arrived as planned with a jeep that belonged to one of his numerous friends. The driver helped load the vehicle with my luggage and we were off. I noticed that he looked a bit pale and I asked if he was all right. He more or less brushed the question off. So, we talked about my birthday, which was coming up that Wednesday, and he said he would try to make the party after work with his wife and daughter. When we arrived at my campus, he helped me unload and put my stuff in my dormitory. I hugged him and thanked him for his help and told him I would see him that Wednesday for my birthday. I did not know that was the last time I would see him alive.

On Tuesday, the day before my birthday, I heard from Frank's wife that he was not feeling well and would not be able to attend the birthday celebrations I had planned for Wednesday. He was going to see the doctor because his feet were swollen, and they would do some tests. At the time I did not think too much of it. It was normal for people to be unwell and go see the doctor, then everything would be fine. I had no idea the seriousness of what my brother was facing combined with the challenges of having a very poor health care system in Sierra Leone.

The next day I still had a few friends round for my birthday, but in the midst of it I received a call informing me that things were really serious with Frank. He needed dialysis, which was not available at that time in Sierra Leone. His kidney had failed and he was in hospital. I could not believe what I was hearing. For some reason it felt as if I were hearing news about somebody else, not the brother who I had just seen, spoken to, and hugged, who had promised to be at my birthday party. *It cannot be. How could things have deteriorated so quickly since the last time I saw him, not even a week before?* These were just some of the thoughts running through my mind.

The birthday celebration was cut short, and we made our way to the hospital. But unfortunately, I could not see him because he had been sedated. The doctors, his wife, and our family discussed the best way forward. I thought about mum who had travelled to England less than a year ago and wondered how she must be feeling. She had been contacted by her sister, my aunt, who was a doctor and understood all the medical challenges Frank was facing.

There was talk at that time of flying him to Ghana, as they had more advanced health care than Sierra Leone. There was also talk of getting a dialysis machine from England, but it needed to be done immediately. Time was of the essence. All these various plans of action were being discussed but none of them could happen immediately, and I thought *I need to pray*. I needed God to come through for us in this time of need. I was still a new believer and I took God at His word. I felt that I had to stand in the gap and pray through the night for Frank to get better, as only God could bring him through this. We were hitting a lot of roadblocks to get him the care that he needed, but God who is the healer would put everything right.

I can remember that Thursday night so vividly. I was staying in my cousin's spare room, as I could not be at university with all this going on. I started praying, speaking to God my Father about Frank and what

I wanted Him to do. I was interceding for a miracle, praying that above all odds Frank would be healed, that this was not the end. I thought about his nine-month-old daughter and his wife; I thought about my mum and our family; I thought about all the talent Frank had and how God could use him further. I had also heard that the pastor who hosted the all-night prayer service my cousin and I had been attending had befriended Frank and his wife and had visited him in hospital. And I prayed, crying to the Lord to heal him. I interceded into the early hours of the morning because I did not feel the peace I craved. I did not yet feel that all would be well, that we would not lose Frank at the young age of twenty-nine, so soon after he had gotten married and had a child. I thought he would pull through. When I had no more tears and my voice was hoarse, I stopped praying and went to bed.

The next morning was a Friday, and I went back to the hospital. I had heard from my aunt that the medical team was going to try something different to help him, so I was hopeful. I really believed that this was the answer to my prayers. I remember pacing outside the ward, praying and trusting God for a miracle.

I will never forget seeing my aunt coming toward us to tell us that Frank was gone. So many emotions went through me. At first I could not say anything. Then I got really angry. I could not believe that God would take him when he had a nine-month-old daughter who needed him. I also felt let down. I had prayed through the night for healing and God had not answered my prayers.

What do you do when you pray and stand on God's word yet it feels as if God has not answered your prayer? The simple answer is that you continue to trust God that He knows best. Though it is hard, and in your heart you feel angry or disappointed, you have to trust God. He knows what is best. We do not have the answers from the master plan. To me, and to most people, it seemed that Frank's life was cut short. But he probably achieved more in twenty-nine years than most people do if they live to be one hundred. We are all here to achieve the purpose God has for us. For some of us, this takes fewer years than it takes for others.

At Frank's funeral it became very clear that he had touched a lot of lives through the numerous organisations he had been part of. He had played clarinet and other instruments as a member of his secondary school's band, and later he had been the organist at a lot of weddings, funerals, choir festivals, and thanksgiving services. He had made himself available to so many churches, choirs, musical groups, and associations. He had also started teaching music to the next generation. It was part of his side hustle, but what he may not have realized at the time is that he was passing on his legacy to future musicians. He was revered at his funeral. There were people of all ages paying homage to how he had positively affected their lives.

3

STANDING ON THE WORD

As a young believer when you have that newborn faith, it can be very hard to understand why God answers some prayers but other prayers don't seem to be answered the way we wanted or requested. I was zealous for the things of God. I believed the verses in the Bible when Jesus said,

> "Until now you have not asked [the Father] for anything in My name; but now ask *and* keep on asking and you will receive, so that your joy may be full *and* complete."
>
> (John 16:24)

I believed that when I prayed and asked God to heal Frank in Jesus's name that it should be done. What I did not grasp or understand was God's will in that situation. I did not understand about God's ways and our ways. As Isaiah 55:8–9 says, "'For My thoughts are not your thoughts, Nor are your ways My ways,' declares the Lord. 'For as the heavens are higher than the earth, So are My ways higher than your ways And My thoughts *higher* than your thoughts.'"

When you put your trust in God and you are knocked back because, in your eyes, your prayer was not answered, it is very hard to move forward if you don't have some understanding of why. I had to understand that, whilst I prayed for Frank to be healed, I did not have the bigger picture; only God had that bigger picture. It took time for me to start to understand that God had a plan for Frank's wife and his daughter that would take them away from Sierra Leone, that this event would trigger plans for them to move to England.

It is understandable that, after Frank's loss, I would be really shaken and would have doubts that God is who He says He is. *How could God let my nine-month-old niece be fatherless and my sister-in-law a widow?* These were some of the questions that I did not have answers to. I did not understand how a loving God could take away someone who was so young and had so much to live for. I was going through the motions of reading my Bible and going to church, but I was angry with God. But that was the plan of the enemy.

I was glad I did not stop going to church or reading my Bible, because it was through this that God was able to take away the anger and disappointment that I had. He reminded me about what had previously stopped me from becoming a committed believer: looking at other people who professed to be believers and seeing that they were not living according to God's word. He reminded me that I had said I would look to Him, and not to others, and this included looking at Frank. I had been setting my heart and my whole perspective around Frank, and that was taking my eyes away from God. As it says in the Bible:

> "Let us run with endurance *and* active persistence the race that is set before us, [looking away from all that will distract us and] focusing our eyes on Jesus, who is the Author and Perfecter of faith [the first incentive for our belief and the One who brings our faith to maturity], who for the joy [of accomplishing the goal] set before Him endured the cross, disregarding the shame, and sat down at the right hand of the throne of God [revealing His deity, His authority, and the completion of His work]."
>
> (Hebrews 12:1–2)

I was fixing my eyes on Frank and not on Jesus. Every time I focused on Frank and his passing and how young he was, I became angry and disappointed. But when I fixed my eyes on Jesus, I remembered that Jesus died for me. He lived on this earth as a man for thirty-three years, and again, in our human thinking, we would say He left too soon, there was more that He could have accomplished. But Jesus had done what He had to do and therefore He had to go. If God could not spare His own son Jesus who was sinless, how could I expect Him to let Frank be here beyond the purpose that God had for him? Frank had accomplished what he was here for, and therefore he passed. He had served his purpose.

The more I fixed my eyes on Jesus, the stronger I got and the more bearable my loss became. I know that God loves each and every one of us, and He loves us more than we love ourselves, more than we love each other. If He did not love us, He would not have sent Jesus, His only son, to die for us. Did I love Frank more than God loved him? Definitely not. Did I want the best plans for Frank more than God? Definitely not. In the Bible it says,

> "For You formed my innermost parts; You knit me [together] in my mother's womb."
>
> (Psalm 139:13)

What does this mean? It means that God knows us. He gave us our DNA. He made us to be who we are and put a plan together for when we would be born and when we will die. He knows us inside out. His plan for us is good:

> "For we are His workmanship [His own master work, a work of art], created in Christ Jesus [reborn from above—spiritually transformed, renewed, ready to be used] for good works, which God prepared [for us] beforehand [taking paths which He set], so that we would walk in them [living the good life which He prearranged and made ready for us]."
>
> (Ephesians 2:10)

God wants us to accomplish that plan because He loves us. He cares. I might not always like the direction that God leads me because I don't see the ending when He starts leading me. But I need to trust His leading, because He cares for me and because His plan for me is always good. He will always lead me in the right path toward what is best for me.

All of us have an earthly father who would, in most cases, care for us and want the best for us, though sometimes we would disagree with him because we want to do things our own way. Yet sometimes, because of his experience, he would know that the decisions we are making are the wrong ones and would try to steer us in the right direction by withholding things from us. A father does not do this because he does not care, but because he can see what lies ahead.

I thought Frank could have accomplished so many wonderful things as a musician. I had an image of him becoming an international musician, touring the world, entertaining audiences in different locations playing Handel's *Messiah*. I had so many wishes for him and now he was gone.

I would like all my friends and family to live long and fulfilling lives, but who determines the length of our time here on earth? Definitely not us. God determines how long we will be here, and it is important that we are living according to His will and His plan for our lives. It starts with believing in the Lord Jesus Christ and what He did at Calvary. Jesus died for our sins, and He died in our place so that if we believed in Him we would not perish but have everlasting life. If you belong to another faith, pray that God speaks to your heart. Let him lead you. If you don't believe that there is a God, then think again, meditate on these words, and listen to what your heart is saying to you.

We are all here on earth to fulfil God's purpose for us. Some of us have a longer time to do this, while others have a shorter time. It is important that, whilst we are here, we live for God, because after this life, there is eternity. I know that there are many beliefs regarding this, but I am holding on to what the Bible says:

> "For God so [greatly] loved *and* dearly prized the world that He [even] gave His [One and] only begotten Son, so that whoever believes *and* trusts in Him [as Savior] shall not perish, but have eternal life. For God did not send the Son into the world to judge *and* condemn the world [that is, to initiate the final judgment of the world], but that the world might be saved through Him."
>
> (John 3:16–17)

I cannot tell you about God's love and how He cares for me without sharing the ultimate sacrifice that God made in letting his one and only Son, Jesus, die for you and me. We are all sinners, and the only sacrifice that could atone for our sins was the death of Jesus. When Jesus died, He paid the price for you and for me. He paid the price for Frank and for everyone who was yet to be born.

My comfort is that I will be reunited in heaven with Frank and all loved ones who died as believers. This is not the end. As it says in the Bible:

> "Jesus said to her, 'I am the Resurrection and the Life. Whoever believes in (adheres to, trusts in, relies on) Me [as Savior] will live even if he dies.'"
>
> (John 11:25)

There is a life better than this. Jesus promises us that, if we believe in Him, though we die in the flesh, we will continue to live, because our spirit leaves this earthly body. We are then reunited with our Heavenly Father. This life is not the end for all of us who believe in Jesus. So, if you are reading this and you have not taken that step of faith yet, this is your opportunity to do so.

4

An Offer I Could Not Resist

Frank's passing triggered a change in my future plans. The following year my aunt decided that it would be good for me to visit my mum in England, as she was grieving for Frank all by herself, without any of her other children with her. She had not come over for Frank's funeral since it is not the custom of Sierra Leoneans for parents to attend the funerals of their children. I think it is the custom for most West African countries that the parents, especially the mothers, do not attend the burials of their children. It had cost a lot of money for her to go to England and she was still in the process of sorting out her late husband's estate. So, it made sense for one of us to go over and spend some time with her.

When my aunt told me that she planned to take me with her during the summer months to visit my mum, my first thought was that I would stay with my mum. I would live with her in England and not come back to Sierra Leone. I had just finished university in Freetown and had earned my degree in Linguistics and Religious Studies. I had not yet applied for any jobs, so it was the ideal time for me to start a new life in another country. There was no promise of a job to keep me in Freetown, so I started seeing this as an opportunity that would open doors for me. I was excited to be going over to see my mum; we were very close and it had been over a year since she had left for England. I remember speaking to her when she learnt that my aunt was bringing me over to see her. She was so excited. She had been so sad after the loss of my brother, so it was a good thing that my aunt came up with this perfect plan.

Before my mum went to England, I was one of few people I knew who had had no desire to live in another country. I had no desire to live in Europe or in America. I had aspirations to travel but not to live abroad. At that time, I loved living in Sierra Leone even though things were not great there and even though I always heard about the opportunities for education and career progress that could be attained in the Western part of the world. Yet during my early teenage years, the idea of leaving did not appeal to me. Perhaps it was because of the high crime rates elsewhere. I constantly heard news of murders and attacks from friends and family who had already left, and it seemed very scary to me.

Apart from the occasional protests against the government, there was nothing scary that happened in Sierra Leone. (Of course, this was way before the tragedy of the guerilla warfare that started in 1997 in Freetown.) Although on one occasion when I used to live with my cousin and his wife and family, there was a coup. He was in the army so we used to live in the army quarters. I remember that we had to be smuggled from the quarters late at night to stay with another relative who lived far away from there. Since at the time my cousin did not know if it would be a peaceful coup, it was important to take precautions and move our family away from the quarters for safety. If it was not peaceful, we would have been in danger. At the time it was a very scary situation, but when we were later told that the coup had been peaceful and all was calm, we moved back to the army quarters. That was my only scary moment when I was in Sierra Leone. I was glad that I was not there when the guerilla war started, as I have heard of so many scary encounters with the rebels and the atrocities that people went through. I do not know how I would have survived that, but God in His mercy brought me over to England so I did not have to go through it.

I also had this wrong idea that believers in very developed countries were not as committed as those of us who were in underdeveloped and developing countries. I believed that our faith was stronger because we did not have access to most things and therefore did not take anything for granted. Whether it was health care, social care, or the higher cost of living, we had to trust God for everything. I have since learnt that there are believers with strong faith and commitment in the western part of the world, just as there were in Sierra Leone before I left. I believe I was still being delivered from the judgemental spirit that had been stopping me from making a commitment to Jesus. There was a part of me that thought I would fall into the trap of depending on material things rather than on Jesus, as had so many of the believers I knew once they left Sierra Leone. I was also concerned that I would not be able to find a Bible-believing church like the one I had been attending and that this would likewise lead to my fall away from grace. When I think of it now, I realised how naïve and uneducated about the churches and believers in the western part of the world I was.

These were the thoughts I had held onto before the grief and the loss and then the opportunity to be reunited with my mum came knocking at my door. There is something you should know about me and my mum: we had a very close relationship. My mum told me that well before she ever got pregnant, she wanted a daughter. Part of the reason was because when she was a teenager, she had been a babysitter for some of the neighbour's children and they were all girls and she had loved taking care of them. When she got married and got pregnant with her first child, she hoped she would have a girl. Six pregnancies later she finally had me, her only daughter. Don't get me wrong; she loved every boy child she had and never showed any favouritism to me over my brothers. But I definitely knew I was loved. At the same time, she did not let me get away with anything. She was a very strict disciplinarian, and I believe that some of that definitely rubbed off me. The thought of living with her again really took away all the negative thoughts I had previously had about being a believer in the western world.

Before she had come over to England, life had been tough for us. There were days when we did not know where our next meal would come from. There were times when Mum had to sell her own clothes to be able to put food on the table for us. She had retired at the age of fifty-five, which, at that time, was the standard age for retirement for government employees in Sierra Leone. She had planned on living on a combination of her retirement payout and income from a hat-making business she had started. Unfortunately, she had had to use most, if not all, of her retirement money on an unexpected situation, which left her without those funds. The demand for hats also dried up, which meant that sales from her custom shop also became unreliable. The two of us had even been given eviction notice because the landlady whose house we were renting wanted it for other uses. When Mum went to England, it was a godsend. Indeed, the Bible says,

> "And we know [with great confidence] that God [who is deeply concerned about us] causes all things to work together [as a plan] for good for those who love God, to those who are called according to His plan *and* purpose."
>
> (Romans 8:28)

God had a plan for us, and that plan was leading to a life away from Sierra Leone. It turned out I would have many more opportunities in England than I would have had in Sierra Leone. I was excited about the future, even though there was so much to do before my departure. For example, I did not have a passport, as I had never gone outside of Sierra Leone before, and there were vaccines to take care of as well. It was painful to say good-bye to my brothers, my close friends, and my grandmother, as I did not know when I would see them again. But this sadness was mixed with the anticipation of flying on an aeroplane for the first time and the joy of reuniting with my mum again. It was a bittersweet but very exciting time for me.

5

Embracing My New Surroundings

I left Freetown, Sierra Leone, on 5 August 1993. After about an hour layover in Amsterdam, I arrived at Heathrow Airport in London on the morning of 6 August 1993, then took a shuttle to Gatwick. I would be staying with another aunt in Surrey for the weekend before making my way to Bedfordshire on the following Monday. I remember speaking to Mum on the phone and feeling so happy because I would be seeing her in a couple of days. It felt surreal to finally be there.

Meanwhile, that Saturday, I had a wedding to attend, along with my cousin who had accompanied me on this trip. We were planning to take the train there and back. My aunt who lived in Surrey was very knowledgeable about what trains we should take and where we should connect, so it was like we had our own personal information board. Unfortunately, in those days there were no mobile phones, so if we got stuck, we would have to find a phone box to make a call. Unlike nowadays, there were still plenty of those around, so it would not be a problem, as long as we had the necessary coins to make the call. How times have changed compared to then; now everyone has a mobile phone with easy access to all train stations, train times, and connections.

My cousin and I dressed in our traditional outfits for the wedding and received repeated instructions from both aunties on what to do and who to talk to if we needed information. I could understand my aunts' concern, as they had promised my mum that we would be with her that coming Monday. And of course, the last thing my aunt wanted was to have to tell Mum that something had happened to me, especially after the loss of my brother. If it had been up to my mum, she would have preferred for us to go directly to Bedfordshire, as she could not wait to see me. But after about the hundredth reminder of what to do and what not do en route, since this was our first time in this strange country, we set off.

It's funny how we use the term "strange" so loosely when we are not familiar with something. Anything that is different or unfamiliar we tend to label as strange. This was an especially common use of the word for those of us from Sierra Leone, particularly in those days.

My auntie had attained her medical qualifications in England and Scotland and went on to become the first female gynaecologist in Freetown, Sierra Leone. She was a member of a few international organisations and was a seasoned traveller. But it was exciting stepping out in England for the first time without her. My cousin and I were two adults; how hard could it be if we followed the clear instructions we had been given? It should be easy peasy. We did make a few wrong turns, and we received some stares from passersby who were not used to seeing people in full African attire, but we eventually found our way to the wedding and enjoyed ourselves.

The bride and groom were Sierra Leoneans, so there were a lot of Sierra Leoneans there. At least we fit in quite well there in our traditional African attire.

On the way back, we had to wait for a while for our train. Since there were two of us, we did not feel too intimidated being on the platform with only a handful of others. Still, because it took a while before the train came, we wondered if it would have been better if we had left a bit earlier, but we had been enjoying ourselves at the wedding. When we got off the train at the end of the journey, we had a bit of a walk before getting back to our aunt's house. But again, because we had each other, it was not so frightening. Our aunts were relieved when we arrived home safely.

I was inwardly satisfied that we had navigated the whole journey on the train without someone else accompanying us. When we came to England, trains and escalators were new phenomena, as we did not have either of them in Sierra Leone. Getting money out of a hole in the wall from a cash machine was likewise unfamiliar. We tried not to look around with wonder and amazement at all the spectacular things that residents of England take for granted.

On Sunday, we went to London for sightseeing. My aunt was familiar with the journey, as it was one she had made several times. My cousin and I could relax and left all the navigation to her. It was great to visit all the famous places that we had heard so much about: Big Ben, Oxford Circus, Harrods, and Buckingham Palace, to name just a few. We did not have time to explore each sight; this was just a chance to see the familiar places that we had heard so much about. I felt at the time that our aunt wanted to see these places through our eyes—not that she was jaded, but because she had been to London so often, it had become overly familiar to her. Whilst for us, this was all very new.

When we boarded the big red double-decker buses, we experienced firsthand the politeness of our fellow passengers. That really made it feel like we were in another world, which, to a certain extent, we were. It was very unusual not to experience a lot of pushing and shoving, as it was the norm in Sierra Leone for everyone to fight their way onto the bus. But in London, people were very well mannered, forming orderly queues to get on the bus. When we needed to get off the bus, we did not have to scream at the top of our voices to let the driver know that we wanted him or her to stop at the next bus stop. All we had to do was press the bell, which would alert the driver that there were passengers who needed to get off at the next stop.

It was also a warm day with lots of people out sightseeing, so we fit in quite well with the other tourists looking with wonder at Big Ben. We had heard so much about this famous sight, and now we got to be there in person, looking at it in awe. I also looked at the pedestrian crossings and zebra crossings with amazement, though I now take them for granted. There were no pedestrian crossings or zebra crossing where I had come from, so this was all a novelty to me.

Even in those first few days, my image and perspective of England started to change. I realised that I had dwelled too much on its negative aspects without considering the positive aspects of what I had heard or been told. As I said earlier, I had had an image of a place full of criminals killing innocent people. I could see then that it was different. One could walk around and do normal things without being killed. There were people who smiled at you and said pleasantries about the weather. I also noticed that people were very willing to help if you needed directions. I also learnt that you needed to receive the directions cautiously, as a five-minute walk for one person could be a thirty-minute walk for me.

Whilst my perspective and idea of England was changing, I still missed the family and friends I had left in Sierra Leone. Yet already I felt that I could make this work. I could make a life here, if that was what God wanted for me.

6

SETTLING IN MY NEW LIFE

On Monday 9 August, my aunt, my cousin, and I travelled by train to Bedfordshire to meet my mum. I was so excited to see her, and she was just as excited to meet with us. It felt as if it had been years since I last saw her, even though it was less than two years. When we got off the train, we took a taxi to the house my mum lived in. I remember how wonderful it was to be hugged by mum. She had put on weight; she looked healthy and so much younger. Life in England had definitely been good for her. Although she had lost Frank, she did not seem worse off in appearance. I knew it was all internal. I was very happy to see her looking so well.

I remember that when we were growing up in Sierra Leone, she would tell us about England. She told us about the politeness and discipline of the people and about all the places she visited whilst she was living there and studying. She had always longed for the life she had left in England. She had craved the anonymity of living there with everyone minding their own business.

During that first week while my aunt and cousin from Sierra Leone stayed in Bedfordshire with us, I also reunited with another very close cousin of mine. I always marvel at how amazing God is, how He brings key people into your life at certain points in time. This cousin, Sophia, had been introduced to us by Frank when we were in Sierra Leone. Frank had first met her while he was out with some friends, and because of the uniqueness of her last name, which was also our mum's last name, he immediately knew that there was a family connection there. He invited her to visit our mum, and this led to a reunion with key members of our family. She became a very important person in all our lives, but especially mine. She even lived with us for a time when we were all in Sierra Leone, and for me it was like having a sister. We could share all sorts of girly stuff about boys that I could not share with my brothers or my mum. We developed a very strong bond that even my mum became a little jealous of. We would go everywhere and do everything together, and we were always whispering and giggling together as teenage girls do. Of course, because we were giggling about stuff mum should not hear, we would immediately go quiet when she was near, and not surprisingly, she was not happy about it. It was really bittersweet for me when Sophia had to return to her home and later on moved to England. I had missed her terribly. To be in the same place with her once again was a godsend. She was the person responsible for Mum moving to Bedfordshire and now also for me making this place my new home.

My aunt and cousin stayed with us for a week before they returned to London, though they would visit us again before going back to Sierra Leone. Mum and I settled into a routine. We were living in a shared house and she was still sorting out financial stuff after the death of her husband.

It did not matter where we were, though, as long as we had each other. And I also had my cousin Sophia, who was now married with a son. I could spend time with her when I needed I change of scenery.

Mum was so happy to introduce me to the members of her church. Whilst she had been in England, she had become a believer and her faith had grown. She had told everyone in church about me and my faith, and I definitely felt that she could not wait to show me off to everyone. I didn't mind as long as it helped her in the grieving process for my brother. She had told me of all the support that she received from the pastor and his wife and the other members of the church. She did not want for anything. There was always someone there to support her.

On Sunday mornings there was someone who would collect us for church, then someone else would take us home. Usually there was also an evening service so someone would collect us for that and would also take us home again. There was a midweek prayer meeting in one of the church members' homes, so there would be someone to give us a lift to that house. There would be someone who would take me to Bible study and take me home afterwards. It was like meeting extended family members that I never knew I had. It definitely gave me a different perspective on what I had thought about the churches and believers in England. The church was Bible believing with committed members. It was not just about the preaching and teaching; their actions showed they were living it. Don't get me wrong; I missed my church in Sierra Leone. I missed the way of life in Freetown, the friends I had left behind, and the members of my family, especially my brother Raymond because we were very close. I remember writing long letters to him about what life was like in England and how I missed my life in Sierra Leone.

A few friends of mine had also moved to England, and I reconnected with them. They lived in London, so I would often go to the city for weekends to have a change of scenery and to be with friends who I had shared a lot with. I was also thinking of my next steps, as I was totally dependent on Mum. She was the sole breadwinner, though I had earned some money-making bridesmaid dresses for one of the ladies who got married soon after I arrived from Sierra Leone. Mum had been blowing my trumpet about how good a dressmaker I was although I had only made two bridesmaid dresses previously in Sierra Leone before I got pulled in to making four bridesmaid dresses of different sizes for people who I barely knew. The pressure was definitely on, as I needed to do something to earn money.

There were a few ladies in church who needed a minder for their young children whilst they were at work. They first approached Mum, who then told me about this opportunity to earn some pocket money. Since I was still unfamiliar with the town, they offered to collect me so I would not have to find my way there and back. And, as they were friends, they would get all the children (seven of them, ranging in age from two to twelve) into one home After a conversation with both families, I agreed and started childminding for them two to three days a week. It was a no-brainer.

It was exhausting, especially chasing after the little ones to make sure that they were safe and keeping them away from danger. In those days there were not so many regulations around childminding at home, so it was easier, though sometimes I had difficulty understanding what the children were saying. I was still trying to get my head around their regional English accent that didn't pronounce the letter *t*.

On some days I helped prepare dinner. Some of the dishes, like leg or shoulder of lamb or beef, were new and unfamiliar to me. My friend would prepare the meat then tell me when to put it in the oven and for how long. Or she would season the meat the night before, so all I had to do was put it in the oven. Then it would be ready when she got home.

Over time my confidence in the kitchen grew, but then I had a setback. My friend had started preparing a traditional Caribbean soup. The meat was still tough and needed more cooking so it could get soft. That was not a problem. If all I had to do was cook it until it was soft, I could do that. But she also wanted me to make dumplings the Jamaican way. First of all, I had never even heard of dumplings that go in soup, so I definitely did not know how to make them. She told me it was easy: flour and water were the key ingredients, to which I would add some sugar, then mould them into a round or oval shape and put them in the pot of soup. I thought, *How hard can this be?* I did not foresee any problems. I thought I had followed the instructions carefully, but the end result was not the same and of course it was difficult to convince the children that these were the dumplings they knew and loved. They looked nothing like their mum's dumplings. They did not have the right shape. From then on I never made dumplings again. Even now, years later, I ask my husband to make dumplings. There are a few other stories like the dumpling episode, and they were good lessons in life skills in my new environment.

In those early days when I could not work officially, as I was on a holiday visa, the money I got from childminding was handy. It enabled me to have some independence and not be totally dependent on Mum for everything. It also increased my knowledge of all the daytime soaps and children's programmes. I became well versed in who was who on *Neighbours* and *Home and Away*, two of the Australian soaps that the children loved watching after school. I also got acquainted with *Byker Grove*, a children's TV series that aired between 1989 and 2006, featuring the duo Ant and Dec who at the time played the characters PJ and Duncan in the series.

Looking back at my brief time as a child minder, I learnt a lot from the two families that helped me when I later became a mum. Their values and the way they did stuff were important life lessons. They had strict routines for the younger ones that I had to adhere to. One of these was making sure that they had afternoon naps, as this prevented them from becoming very irritable around dinnertime. It was foreign to me to put a child to bed when they were not sleepy. But I trusted their judgement as parents and followed their routine, and I was pleasantly surprised that the young ones did go to sleep. There were three of them under the age of five; the other four were in school so I only watched them after school when they got dropped off by one of the parents who had a flexible shift as a dental nurse.

I will always be grateful to both families for trusting me with their precious children in those early days. I was practically a stranger when I first started, with no formal education on childminding. They knew my mum, and the same trust they had in her they likewise bestowed on me, her daughter. They also bought me my first winter coat. I had arrived in

England during the summer, but it was autumn when I started childminding, with winter fast approaching. In those days it was bitterly cold with freezing temperatures and a lot of snow. I had been wearing one of Mum's winter coats, which was functional, but not many young women in their twenties would have been caught dead in it. I did not care—or I thought I did not, until I received my brand-new coat. Then I saw the difference.

After five months of childminding, I applied for and was granted a two-year working visa. In those days the UK government would give working visas to citizens of a commonwealth country. I hoped to get an office job with the degree I had from home, but nothing was forthcoming. I registered with an agency and did temporary work for another three months, which helped me get very familiar with the roads and streets, as I was always the last one to be dropped off by the agency's minibus. I was fascinated by the different names of the routes, trying to understand the difference between an avenue, a drive, and a way, since these terms were unfamiliar to me. After three months of working in different places, I finally secured a permanent staff position as a packer at a tablet manufacturing and packaging company.

One of the things that stood out for me after working in so many different environments was how normal it was for people to swear. I was not used to this. I don't remember the people around me using profanities willy-nilly in normal conversation when I was in Sierra Leone. I had never sworn, and I didn't understand why sometimes every other word in someone's conversation was a swear word. I struggled with it. It really disturbed my spirit being around people who swore all the time. After a few months of working there, I had to say something. The colleagues I worked with had noticed that I don't swear, and they wanted to know why. This was my first opportunity to share my faith with them.

Most of them were older than me and had worked there for years, some of them for more than twenty years. As time passed, they accepted that I was different, that I was a believer, so most of the older ones would refrain from swearing if I was around or near them. I would share about church and God when the opportunity arose. I also realised that a very common topic of discussion, apart from the weather, was about what would you be doing at the weekend. As soon as it was coming to the end of the working week, that would be the question that would be asked by anyone whom I was working with. Of course, my weekend always involved church, so I would use that opportunity to plant seeds of faith. Some would listen and ask more questions; some had concluded that it was "one of those happy-clappy churches" and would avoid asking me anymore questions about church. My purpose was not to "save" anyone, as only God could do that. My purpose was to plant seeds and to lead a life that was a testimony of a believer in Christ. I believed that God would do the rest.

One of the things I was quickly learning at that time was that most people who I came across in the working environment did not go to church, did not have anything to do with church, and moreover did not even believe that there is God. This was a shock to me, as everyone that had crossed my path in Sierra Leone believed in God. They may have been a Christian, a Muslim, or a Jehovah's Witness, and even if they were not one of those, they still believed there was a God. Being around people who did not believe at all was new for me. I realised in those early days that only God can give someone the revelation of who He is. I could only sow seeds of faith and share my testimony of how I came to be a believer.

I felt that I left a good impression of a believer. In fact, after I left that job to go back to college for additional education, I would meet a few of them in later years, and they were very happy to see me and would ask me about church. I continue to remember them in prayer, asking that God would reveal Himself to them and that the seeds of faith I planted in them would be watered by someone else.

7

SETTLED BUT UNSETTLED

Four years later, I had definitely settled into the British way of life. I could understand the regional accent where I lived much better though I still struggled with other regional accents (for example, the Liverpool accent). Before coming over I did not know that not everyone spoke the Queen's English. It was an interesting discovery to find out that there were so many different accents in England and across the whole UK.

Mum and I were finally living in a spacious, two-bedroom flat in a very nice area in Bedfordshire. This was our fourth accommodation since I had arrived in England, and I loved it. It was quite close to the town centre but also in a quiet residential area. Before that, I had experienced all the different types of living accommodations one could experience. We lived in a shared flat for about a month before we moved to a studio flat. Though at the time I was just grateful that we no longer had to share our cooking and bathroom space with anyone else, we could not stay there as it was so draughty. We were not there long before we also noticed that there was a lot of mould in the studio. We realized this was the reason it was cheaper than the other places Mum had viewed. She thought she had got a bargain. It appeared the owners had not addressed the underlying issue; instead, they had just put on a fresh coat of paint to disguise what was underneath. It was a lesson in how someone could dress up nicely and look good on the outside, but their heart could be bad.

A few weeks after that, we had to move again. This time it was to a one-bedroom flat with separate kitchen, living area, and bedroom. It was not a problem that I was still sharing a bedroom with my mum. It was a new build, so it was very clean with no mould or draught. After we had been there for a year, my late stepfather's estate was finally sorted and we could now afford to live in a spacious two-bedroom apartment. Finally, I could have my own bedroom with my own bed. I felt settled.

My two-year working visa was coming to an end. I had decided that I wanted to do something more, and the only way I could do that was to go back to school and get the kind of qualifications that would be recognised in UK. I had done an access course at one of the local colleges, so now I had the qualifications to go to university as a mature student.

Whilst a few people told me that, because I already had a degree from Sierra Leone, I could apply to do my master's, I had no idea what I should be doing my master's in. I did not want to continue with Linguistics or Religious Studies; I wanted to do something different, something that would get me into a corporate environment. I had done well in A Level Economics whilst I was in sixth form, but I had not gotten good enough grades in Mathematics at O Levels to get me into the business field at university. But now with my new access, I could get into the business field. I was very much interested in Marketing.

Everything was looking good; I was now at university. I was looking forward to what the future might hold after I completed my marketing degree in three years at the University of Bedfordshire (previously known as the University of Luton).

Sometimes it may seem as if everything is going well, then suddenly it is not. What you least expect happens, and life as you know it changes. Then things are never the same as before. Don't get me wrong; whilst some events are life changing, they also shape you into the person that you need to be for your next step. At the time you are going through a life-changing event, you are not aware that you are developing attributes that will make you a better person. We prepare to take tests and exams at school that will show we are ready for the next step in our education, or we finish a project or secondment at work to show that we are ready for the next step in a career. It is similar in life: we go through trials and tests, and when we come through, we look back and see that our character has developed. We have more patience or endurance than before.

I never expected that life would change drastically in my fifth year of living in England. My faith in God was strong. I was very much involved in the youth and women's ministry at my local church. God had created opportunities for me to share His Word on a number of occasions. I had been pleasantly surprised that God could use me as a communicator in our church. I was also leading Sunday school for some of the youth.

In the summer before I started university, I noticed my mum was complaining about being constipated and not having regular bowel movements as she should. She did not think it was anything serious, so she took laxatives and ate more fruits and other food that would help give her regular bowel movements. After some weeks she had not said anything more about it, so I thought all was well. Unbeknown to me, she had made an appointment with her doctor, and the doctor had referred her to the hospital to see a consultant. She had already seen the consultant, who had done some tests without my knowing.

The first I found out about this development was when she got a call from the consultant to give her the results of the test and she was told that she should attend the consultation with someone else. Mum had no other choice but to tell me that she had been concerned enough with the continuous constipation that she had seen her doctor. He had then referred her to the hospital, and she needed me to go with her for another appointment with the consultant. Although I was shocked that she had kept all of this to herself, it was not surprising. Mum was a very private person and would only share personal things if she had no other choice. I trusted God that all would be well. I knew what my mum was like. She had been like that all her life, and I did not expect her to change in her later years. I was glad the consultant had asked her to bring someone, as this meant I could ask all the questions and would get all the information we needed.

I was not prepared for what the consultant told us once we got to his office at the hospital. We were both unprepared for it. It was like having a flashback to when I was eleven years old, but worse.

Back in Sierra Leone, my mum had had a big celebration for her fiftieth birthday, which was unlike her, as she was otherwise very conservative.

After the party she started experiencing severe constipation. Not only was she having constipation, but she was also losing weight rapidly and her stomach was protruding as if she were pregnant. I was eleven years old at the time and actually thought that I was getting another sibling; I always equated a protruding stomach with a baby. Shortly after this, my eldest brother (whom I had never met because I was born after he had left for Germany to study medicine) made arrangements for Mum to travel to Germany to have an operation. He was now a qualified doctor and was practising at the hospital where Mum would be admitted. Mum had a tumour in her stomach, which is why she was unwell. I did not know any of this until much later. At the time, I was just told that she was unwell and that the treatment she needed could only be done overseas. That was my first indication that Sierra Leone's health care system was inadequate, if people had to leave Sierra Leone to get medical help.

She was successfully treated in Germany and stayed there for about six months under the care of my brother. She had to recuperate thoroughly before she could be signed off from the hospital. She came back home with a scar that was the whole length of her stomach. She would share with us how long the operation was and all the details of the care she had to get afterward. Thankfully she had been told that the tumour was benign.

Here we were almost twenty years later, being told that the tumour was back, but this time it was not benign. The test result from the biopsy had shown it was cancer. That six-letter word that no one wants to hear. Being a believer, I was hopeful. I thought, *We are no longer in Sierra Leone; we are in England where there is a more than adequate health care system.* She would be fine. She had defeated this tumour before and she would defeat it again. I tuned out the conversation for a few seconds as my mind wandered off. I was jolted back to the present when I heard the word "spread." I had to ask the consultant to recap what he had said. He said, "I am sorry, but the cancer has spread." It was now inoperable, which meant it was terminal. Mum started crying. This strong woman whom I had known all my life, who held in her emotions in public, really fell apart in that consultation room after hearing the news that the cancer was inoperable. I was devastated. As the news sunk in, I also started crying. I forgot that I was supposed to be there to comfort her. But honestly I don't know who was comforting who, as we were both crying in front of the consultant. He gave us some tissues and time to calm our emotions before he told us the next steps. Next steps involved chemo and radiotherapy to extend her life for a few months. Basically, we were being told that mum had less than a year to live.

How could this be? Why would this happen just when we were finally settled? I was just about to start university. I had successfully been given a grant for the fees; even though in those days going to university was free for citizens, because I was not a citizen, I had to pay. But as I had been living in the county for the last three years, I was not technically considered a foreign student. I received an exemption from the fees that foreign students who had only just arrived would have had to pay.

In those early days I could not get my head around the news that I was going to lose my mum. This would be different from losing Frank, as the grieving process started as soon as I heard the words "cancer" and "inoperable." It was as if the consultant had told me that Mum was dead. Neither of us could believe it. It was hard to plan for the future knowing that Mum would not be with me for much longer.

Mum was constantly crying when it was just the two of us. This made me really sad. Over time I realised that it was normal that your parents pass before you, so I had to be strong for her.

In the midst of my grief, I also had this irrational anger directed at my mum or God, I was not sure at the time. I felt that I had only had a short time with my mum. *If only she had had me when she was younger* was one of my selfish thoughts. Then we would have had longer together. She would have lived to see my children, her grandchildren. I would cry, "Lord, why was I not born when my mum was in her thirties so we could have had longer?" It was irrational when I thought about it later, but at the time I needed to release my emotions. This anger against my mum and against God seemed relevant to me.

8

SURPRISES AND CHALLENGES

It was only a few months before that that we had celebrated Mum's seventieth birthday. It had been a very quiet one since she did not want any fuss. As we approached the big day, I had asked her what she wanted to do and had suggested a party, which she immediately declined. She told me she wanted it to just be us: me, her, my adopted sister, Sophia and her family (there were now four of them), and Frank's daughter who would be coming up from London with her mum.

I discussed with my sister-in-law, my cousin Sophia, and my adopted sister who lived in Hounslow how I wanted to hold a small surprise party for Mum's seventieth birthday. They all agreed that it would be great to do something to celebrate this significant milestone. Together with close family and friends, we planned the day. A close friend of hers from another church took her out for the morning whilst, together with a few helpers, I put up banners and balloons. We had also got a cake, as no birthday party would be complete without a birthday cake and candles. I had deliberated on whether or not to have balloons with her age on them; Mum was very particular about whom she shared personal details with, especially her age.

But I did not think she would mind, as these were all people who were very close to her who would know how old she was anyway.

She was pleasantly surprised when she arrived home with her friend who had kept her occupied whilst we decorated the flat. There were less than twelve people there, all very close family and friends with whom she was happy to share her birthday. We had cooked our traditional food, jollof rice with chicken stew, and made the usual drinks, homemade ginger beer. As a Sierra Leonean from the Krio ethnic group, there was no way you could have a celebration without jollof rice and homemade ginger beer. Although she had said she did not want a fuss, she really enjoyed the low-key celebration. We spent time reminiscing about Sierra Leone, we took photos for the memory book, and we made a lot of phone calls home. We did not realize at the time how significant this celebration was. I am always telling people to enjoy and treasure the present moment with loved ones, because we do not know what might happen tomorrow. Tomorrow is not guaranteed.

We never knew that this would be her last birthday with us. Just a few months later we received the appalling diagnosis that she had terminal cancer and had less than a year to live. She had to start chemotherapy immediately to reduce the speed at which the cancer was spreading. She would have to have the chemo at the Mount Vernon hospital, but it was not close to us. Because she did not want many people to know what was going on, we had to depend on transportation provided by the local authority. At this time only our pastor and his wife were aware of her diagnosis. She had sworn me to secrecy. I was not to tell any of the family in Sierra Leone that she had cancer. She would tell them when she was ready.

To prepare her for the chemotherapy sessions, we had to visit the hospital in Mount Vernon before she actually started the treatment. The nurse who was supporting us told us it would be good for her to take up this offer so that she would know exactly what was happening and where. We went down the week before she started the chemo. It seemed like a long journey from where we lived, even though it was less than an hour's drive. When we arrived, we were shown the room where the chemo would be done and also told how long it would take. Mum and I definitely did not like the smell of the anaesthetic, the usual hospital smell of sickness and death. It was good to make this visit, but it also brought home the reality of Mum's illness. Soon she would look like some of the patients we saw whilst we were being shown around. People with no hair, people looking sick and being sick. On the journey back home, we were both very quiet. The visit had confirmed that there were some tough days ahead.

Before the diagnosis she had discussed observing the upcoming fifth anniversary of Frank's passing with my sister-in-law. She was not going to let the cancer diagnosis stop her. She started making preparation for my brother's anniversary memorial. In October of that year, it would be five years since we lost Frank. I went along with it, as it gave her something to take her mind off her predicament. Together with our pastor and his wife, we were believing God for a miracle. I was holding on to the verses in the Bible where it says

"Who has believed [confidently trusted in, relied on, and adhered to] our message [of salvation]? And to whom [if not us] has the arm *and* infinite power of the Lord been revealed?"

(Isaiah 53:1)

The gospel song from Ron Kenoly was also very popular around this time: "Whose report will you believe?" / "We shall believe the report of the Lord."

I was definitely choosing to believe the report of the Lord, not what the report from the consultant had said. I believed that Mum would live beyond the time frame given by the report. Don't get me wrong; I do believe in science and all that the medical world has to offer. But I also believe that the brains and knowledge that they have, they received from God. Therefore, God has the final say. So, I would listen to the doctors, trusting that God could guide them to administer the right treatment. But I also believe that only God knows when we will leave this earth. No matter what the medical people said, I would always look to God for His direction. He has the final say.

I remember how sick Mum was after the first chemo session. I wondered how something that made her feel so sick could be any good for her. For a few days after the session, she would throw up a lot. She would be very sick before she would start to feel better. I cannot remember how many sessions she had during that summer. She still had not yet shared with family in Sierra Leone how sick she was. On the outside she looked the same, so no one could tell that something was wrong when she was not throwing up. If she was feeling better, she would go to church with me. It was around this time that I met Trevor.

One of my mum's biggest fears about her diagnosis was that I was the only one of her children in England whilst all her other children were in Sierra Leone. My three older brothers, including the one who qualified as a doctor in Germany, were now in Sierra Leone. She kept thinking about her imminent death and how I would be left on my own with none of my siblings nearby. I caught her crying a few times when she thought I was still out, and I knew immediately that's what she was thinking. She admitted it on one such occasion. She would have me in tears, because I knew she would not be here when I met someone, got married, and had children. Though she had grandchildren from my older brothers, she had been praying ever since I had come to England to live with her that I would meet someone who I would eventually marry.

I first met Trevor at a barbecue that I did not want to go to. I had just come home from my part-time job at one of the shops in the mall. I was tired, but I had promised my friend Jacqueline that I would cook some jollof rice for her nephew's first birthday party. The celebration was a barbecue at her cousin's house, and I had to keep my word. Mum was over the moon when I told her later that weekend that I had met someone, and that he wanted to meet with her.

In the weeks that followed, she got to know Trevor very well. It's as if we had known Trevor for much more than just a few weeks. Mum felt comfortable with him and would call him if she needed something. It was strange that she did not hesitate to share with him—someone who had just come into our lives—that she was not well, whilst her sisters and children in Sierra Leone had no idea about the magnitude of her illness. She would reach out to Trevor if she had the craving to eat certain food, and Trevor would get it for her since he had a car and could easily pick up things that she needed. Trevor was so good with my mum. He embraced her as if they had known each other for years and not just a few months. Mum told him about her plans for the five-year anniversary memorial for my brother and extended an invitation for him to attend. He accepted.

For someone who was not familiar with our food and traditions, he was amazing. I had thought that he might not come because he was a bit of an introvert and this was a biggie. There were family and friends from London who had come for the memorial cook-up. He had previously met my cousin Sophia but not any other family members. He would be coming on his own and meeting all these people for the first time, most of whom are from Sierra Leone and would be speaking our native dialect Krio. Honestly I did not think he would make it. But then he really surprised me. He came and did not hesitate to sit on the carpet after we had run out of enough chairs with so many people in the flat. He felt right at home and fit right in with our family and friends. I did not know at the time that he was out of his comfort zone, though over the years of being married to him, I realized how he had pushed through his discomfort to be there. He ate all the food offered to him even though this was the first time he was trying some of the different dishes. This made mum very happy. I was quite pleased as well, as it indicated that we would get on.

9

First and Last Christmas

As we approached Christmas 1997, it became obvious to everyone that Mum was not well. She had lost a lot of weight. Previous Christmases she and I had spent the day with my cousin Sophia and her family. We would visit her church then have Christmas dinner with them all afterward. But since this was the first Christmas after meeting Trevor, we decided to do something different. Mum was not up to visiting anyone, so Trevor came to our home first to spend some time with Mum and me. Then he and I went off to Sophia's and later to his parents' house. All his sisters and his brother would be there with their partners, along with lots of visiting nieces and aunties and cousins. It was a great time for me to meet the close family, as I had already met his parents.

It was a really bittersweet time for me. I had Trevor in my life and things were going well with us and this was our first Christmas together. But even though I was trusting God for Mum to be healed, I was also thinking this could be our last Christmas together. It was hard. How could I enjoy my first Christmas with Trevor when this could be my last Christmas with Mum? At this time, she still had not told the family in Sierra Leone about her cancer, and it was weighing heavily on me. At that time the rebel war was in full force in Sierra Leone and all international flights had been suspended. When we had calls from my aunts and my brothers, she would put on a brave front and would speak in a very cheerful voice so that none of them were any the wiser.

At the start of 1998, she was now on radiotherapy. This was really putting a strain on her immune system, so I encouraged her once again to tell her sisters, starting with my aunt who had brought me over to England. I made the call, and Mum told her sister. They decided not to tell their mum, my grandmother, as she was very old and would have been very upset. She had been very upset when Frank passed. I made the call to my brothers, and they were all devastated, especially when I told them the cancer had spread and it was terminal. It was a really sad day for us. At this time most of the church family knew, as Mum was not going to church anymore. The pastor's wife whom she was close with would visit her and share the Bible with her. She would also put on some of the gospel songs we sang in church so that spiritually she was still being fed. We also had lots of video and tape recordings of our church services that she could listen to.

I had thought the chemo sessions were bad, but the radiotherapy sessions were even worse. They left her really sick. The radiation made her incontinent, so she had to use surgical pads. She was becoming really skinny. Sometimes I would look at her and could not recognise this woman who used to be very voluptuous with a great figure. She had become skin and bones, and it was heartbreaking. With tears she would tell me about what she wanted for her funeral service, and I was of two minds. I did not want to talk about it, but yet I needed to know what her final wishes were. It was devastating. She had already spoken to a close family friend in Houston, Texas, who would send the dress she wanted me to lay her in. It was so sad. When the dress arrived, I took it out of the packaging so she could see what it looked like, and she loved it. There were parts of this that were surreal for me, as I could not believe that my mum would not be here to see me finish university, get married, or have children.

Because she knew she would not be here to see my children, she would talk to me about how I should not forget our customs and upbringing. She would tell me that some of us who were born in Sierra Leone or in other African countries forget our upbringing and would bring up our children according to Western ways. She would go on about respecting elders and letting children being children without allowing the child to rule the home. I don't know what her reference point was, but she was keen on driving into me that I must ensure my future children would be respectful and know how to address elders. They were not to address people who could be their parents by their first names. I was also to make sure that they would not take things for granted and that they would start doing little chores when they were small. She kept quoting from this verse in the Bible:

> "Train up a child in the way he should go [teaching him to seek God's wisdom and will for his abilities and talents], Even when he is old he will not depart from it."
>
> (Proverbs 22:6)

"If you start when they are small, showing them what is right from wrong and letting them know they will not get away with bad behaviour, then it will be easier when they are older," she said. As I said before, even though I was the daughter she had longed for, Mum never let me off easily if I had behaved badly or done something wrong. There was no way I would bring up my own children in a different way. I would reassure her time and again that I would remember what she had said—and that I would not just remember it but would do what she had been drilling into me.

I was still going to university, holding down two part-time jobs, and looking after Mum during this time. When I think back on what I went through, I know that it could only be God who saw me through. He knew how hard the coming days were going to be, so He brought Trevor into my life at the right time. If I needed to go anywhere, he would take me. He would pick me up from the shop in the mall after my late shifts, especially during winter when the evenings got dark early, and then he would drop me off at home. Whilst I was doing my part-time hours in the evening, if Mum needed anything, he would get it for her. I felt really supported by him. My mum had indicated that she would like to have a private conversation with him one day when he came round to visit. After they had the conversation, which I was not part of, I noticed that Mum seemed a bit more relaxed. To this day Trevor has not shared with me what Mum said to him in that private conversation a few months before she passed.

As the cancer was progressing and she was on very strong drugs, she would get very sleepy. It was around this time that I started receiving outside support from the MacMillan Cancer Support nurses as well as from two sisters from church. Mum, being the private person that she was, only wanted a few people to be with her if I had to be away. My friend Jacqueline was one of them along with another older sister from church.

It was very difficult for me when I went to church, as everyone wanted to know how Mum was. I would be repeating the same thing over and over again to five, six, or seven different people, and it became very exhausting. I would have preferred if some people apart from just the pastor and his wife would have called during the week to find out how Mum was, instead of waiting until I was in church on Sunday. I started going to church just in time for the service to start and then leaving before the closing prayer. I could not take it anymore. It was so hard to be repeating the same thing over and over again. In those days there was no WhatsApp, and mobile phones were not as common as they are now. It would have been easier to have a WhatsApp group in which I could update everyone who needed to know the latest about Mum.

The Macmillan nurses were visiting us regularly, and they had been talking to Mum about going to a local hospice for a night or two to give me respite. They told her that the change of scenery would also be good for her. It took a lot of convincing for her to agree to try it. She was very reluctant to do it, mainly because she was now very skinny and had a fear of passing away while she was outside her home. Whereas I preferred for her to be in the hospice when she passed; it would have been too much for me to handle if I was all by myself. I told her to try it for one day and if she did not like it, she would not need to go again. She did it, and all went well. I would not say that she loved it, but when she went, she met other people in the same situation as her and I thought it helped her. She did not feel so alone in this sickness. With the help of the nurses at the hospice, she also spent time crafting a lovely tray that featured a beautiful picture of flowers. She was so proud of herself for making it. When I visited her, she showed it off to Trevor and me. I remember holding the tray and thinking *this will be with me forever*. My mum had always been great with her hands, and until her dying days, she was using her talent to make something that would be part of her legacy. I have kept it and use it even to this day.

10

SAYING GOOD-BYE TO MUM

Mum was now much weaker and often very sleepy, as the drugs were increased to reduce her pain and discomfort. She was spending more time at the local hospice, and I was slowly beginning to accept that any time now I would get a call informing me that she had passed. It was really hard for me. After she finally told my aunt in Sierra Leone, she also gave her permission to inform the other aunties in London. The auntie who we had stayed with when I first arrived in England told me that she wanted to visit her. I was not too sure whether Mum would be open to the idea of a visit. To my surprise she agreed. My auntie came from London with two of her sisters to see Mum at the hospice. One of them had been my mum's bridesmaid when she had gotten married, so they were really upset. She asked me why I had not said anything earlier. I could only tell her that Mum did not want a fuss and had not wanted anyone to know. To a certain extent they understood, but I could sense that they were not happy that they had only been informed when she was more or less on her last days. I could also understand things from my mum's perspective, given that, even when she was healthy, it was not as if we had regularly visited our family in London or vice versa.

It is very important that, when everything is going well, we show love and care to those that are dear to us. We should not wait until they are sick or on their deathbed. Most people only want close people around them when they are on their deathbed. They are usually vulnerable and not looking their best, so there is always a fear that anyone who comes close to them when they are in that state are only doing so with ulterior motives. In some cases, this is true. When you are in that phase of illness, the person who is sick wants to have some amount of control over the narrative. You do not want people exaggerating how bad you look just to tell a "good sad" story. The only way to accomplish this is, usually, to limit the amount of people who visit you during that phase. Not that my aunties were people who would do something like that, but Mum was very cautious. She did not agree to visits from many people.

Nowadays there are more treatments available, and recovering from cancer has a higher rate than twenty-six years ago. Even so I do come across people who still want to keep it quiet and only inform a few close people that they are getting treatment for cancer. I think it's because most people associate cancer with death, so once you got it, there was this belief that you would not recover. I think people want to avoid being pitied by others. If the person who is sick is trusting God for healing, telling the wrong person could bring all kinds of unconscious negativity. People might want to tell you about someone else they knew who died of cancer. If it is same type of cancer that the sick person is suffering from, this is not helpful to the sick person's ability to believe in and trust God for a miracle.

When my brother was sick in hospital, it had been unexpected. I had always thought that he died too soon. But in the situation with my mum, I was a little bit more accepting of her forthcoming passing. Still, it did not happen overnight. When I think back on it, I think it's because we had celebrated her seventieth birthday and in the Bible it does say,

> "The days of our life are seventy years—Or even, if because of strength, eighty years; Yet their pride [in additional years] is only labour and sorrow, For it is soon gone and we fly away."
> (Psalm 90:10)

I was trusting God for a miracle, but at the same time trusting that He knows best. My sadness was more selfish, as I thought about all the things that she would miss concerning me. I was in my first year at university, and I thought she would not be here to see me complete my schooling and graduate. She would not see any children that God would bless me with. I had seen how she had taken care of her grandchildren from my brothers, and I was sad that she would not be here for mine.

Her passing was peaceful. I had gone there the evening before, and she was sleeping. I stayed with her for a while, watching her, with tears in my eyes, breathe in and out, wondering if this would be the last time I saw her breathing. It was really sad. Trevor was also with me, and over the last few months, I could see that, even though he had not known my mum for long, she had definitely made an impact on him. He kept telling me that he could not believe how the sickness had progressed so quickly. He could not stay in the room. He had to wait for me outside in the car because it made him too emotional seeing my mum like that. As much as I hated being there, because all around me I saw other patients in different stages of passing from this life in such a very depressing scene, I could not stay away. When I was ready to leave, I took her hands in mine and told her that I loved her. What else could I say, apart from letting her know that she was loved and that I promised I would remember all the advice she had given me and the wisdom she had passed to me over the years.

Early the next morning, which was a Thursday, I got a call from the hospice, and I immediately knew that Mum had passed. I was not surprised when they told me that she had passed early that morning; one of the nurses had been with her at the time. She said I could come to the hospice to collect her things, and if the death certificate was ready, I could take it to the registration office. I felt alone even though I knew I was not alone. I had lovely people around me who were supporting me, but they were not my mum. It was really hard. Even years later, I still miss her. There is a bond between a mother and her child that is very strong. The bond between mum and I had been very strong indeed.

I recalled three other occasions when I had been apart from my mum. The first was when I was about five years old and she had left us to further her studies in England. She was away for two years, and all I could remember from those days was how sad I was. The aunt who I was staying with only had to call me by name and I would start crying because I was missing my mum so much. When she returned from England and we were all back together, it was such a relief. She had missed us also and vowed that she would not leave us behind the next time she had to go away. The next time we were apart was when I was about eleven years old and she had to go to Germany for the operation to remove the tumour in her stomach. She was gone for about six months and again it was hard. The third time was when she came over to England whilst I was in my early twenties, and we were separated for just over a year before I joined her there. It does not matter who else you have in your life; they could be a lovely person, a mother figure, but they can never replace your birth mother once you have developed that bond together.

And I was now experiencing the separation that was final on this earth. I did believe that we would meet again, but it would be in another place, not here on earth, so it was really hard.

When I went to the hospice to collect her stuff, it was with mixed feelings. I was relieved that I would not have to come to the hospice again to see my mum in the condition that really depressed me. This was not because she was not taken care of at the hospice—quite the opposite. She was pampered and looked after very well. The depressing thing for me is that it was where she lost more weight and became almost skin and bones. It was where I saw her confined to a bed, not able to sit on a chair anymore. It was where I saw her drifting in and out of consciousness, barely able to acknowledge that I was there. It was the place where every day someone else who I'd gotten used to seeing would be gone by the next time I visited, which reminded me that soon that would be Mum, here today but gone tomorrow. So yes, I was relieved, but with that relief came the sadness that I was there for the last time to collect her belongings as well as the death certificate. The death certificate was a symbol of finality. A person who was so full of life is gone. No more would you see them laughing or hear the sound of their voice. It was the end. They had passed from this life. It was really hard.

I trusted God to be my father and mother as he promised in the Bible:

> "A father of the fatherless and a judge *and* protector of the widows, is God in His holy habitation."
>
> (Psalm 68:5)

I was fatherless and now motherless. God would look after me. I trusted Him to give me the strength because He cares for me. He knows exactly how much I can take and will not give me more than I can bear. This He says in these verses in the Bible:

> "No temptation [regardless of its source] has overtaken *or* enticed you that is not common to human experience [nor is any temptation unusual or beyond human resistance]; but God is faithful [to His word—He is compassionate and trustworthy], and He will not let you be tempted beyond [to resist], but with the temptation He [has in the past and is now and] will [always] provide the way out as well, so that you

will be able to endure it [without yielding, and will overcome temptation with joy]."

(1 Corinthians 10:13)

God knew exactly how much I could take; He knows how strong I am and how weak I am at the same time. Some people get a diagnosis and the time until their passing could be short; sometimes it could take weeks. God knew that I was not strong enough at that time to cope with a sudden death like my brother's passing. So, in this situation, I had months to prepare myself and learn to accept it, to get stronger emotionally so that I could bear it when Mum passed. The above verse is definitely true in my situation; I needed time before she passed to adjust to what life would be like without Mum.

11

Planning Mum's Service

I had never been involved in planning a funeral before, and I did not know where to start. I had only been living in England for five years, so I still did not know how to navigate such things. The Macmillan nurses and the staff at the hospice were really great in supporting me. They gave me a list of the local funeral services and walked me through what the process would be. Three of my close friends who had also been close to my mum came to spend some time with me. My cousin Sophia who lived locally was also there to support me. And of course, Trevor took time off to be our chauffeur, driving us everywhere we needed to go to put the plans in motion for the funeral.

At least I did not have to think about what Mum would wear, as this had already been decided before she passed. I only had to hand it over to the funeral home. I had to speak to my pastor and his wife regarding the date of the funeral service and where we could have the service. We did not have a building of our own for a worship service, as we used to hire one of the meeting rooms in the town hall and we could not use this for the service. We were affiliated with one of the local churches, which was a Church of

England, and we were quite familiar with the vicar there. It was decided that this would be a fitting venue to hold the service.

With the help of family and friends who knew Mum very well, we put together the hymns and songs that she would have liked. I knew one or two that she had always been humming or singing since we were children, so both those and a few more contemporary songs she had grown to love were added. When we were talking about her impending passing, we had not gone into details about what songs and hymns she wanted for her funeral. At that point I would not have been able to bear it. Though she was emphatic that she did not want to be taken home to Sierra Leone for burial. That and what she would wear were the things that she had been very clear about.

Once I had decided which funeral home we would use, we had to have a meeting to choose the coffin. It is such a daunting experience, especially when you are doing it for the first time. I had hoped that my aunt who had first brought me over would be able to come to England for the funeral so I could have an older family member, and someone who was also close to Mum, to support me. I thought I needed someone that I could lean on. Unfortunately, during this time, the airport was still closed to international flights as the rebel war was still raging on. I could only lean on God. There were no close family members apart from my cousins, aunties from London, and close family friends in attendance. All of this was quite new for Trevor also, so he could only support me by being available to take me where we needed to go. Since the planning did involve a lot of driving, I was grateful that God had brought him into my life when He did.

Eight days later, we had the funeral for Mum. It was a Friday. I had agreed with the funeral directors that we wanted her to be brought to the house where the coffin would be opened for viewing, as this was our custom. I needed to do video recordings for the family in Sierra Leone, since, as I said, they were not able to come over due to the war there. Whilst it would likely not be easy viewing for them, the least I could do was give them the choice of watching the recording or not, which I would send to them at a later date. If I had not recorded it, I would have taken that choice away from them. There was a lovely brother in church who had kindly offered to do the recording, as he videotaped most of our Sunday services and special events. Luckily that was now something else that I did not have to think about.

We had not thought too clearly about the logistics of getting the coffin into our two-bedroom flat. Although we lived on the ground floor, it proved to be a challenge. I am sure the funeral directors later made sure to amend their consultation pack by adding the question, "Could we visit the home before bringing the coffin there on the day?" But they made it work, so anyone who had not seen Mum for a while had the choice of coming to the house an hour before the service to see her laid out in the lovely dress she had requested from our family friend in America. She looked very peaceful in the coffin. She did not look like the skin and bones she had been in the last week before she passed.

Mum had also requested that we would not wear black to her funeral. She had told me that she would prefer if we wore white. This is mainly for the women; the men were not expected to wear white. It is the custom in

Sierra Leone, and definitely for the Krio ethnic group who we belong to, to always choose a colour, and on some occasions even choose the fabric, that the close family will wear as a sign of togetherness and identification. I did not want to do that, so I chose a two-piece white suit for myself and for my adopted sister. I did inform all the female friends and relations that we would wear white. I also chose black hats to wear with the outfit.

I was going through the motions, as I was all cried out. I was in the midst of people who loved me but still felt as if I were on my own. I can only put that feeling down to the fact that no other person, no friend or family member, could share in the emotions that I was feeling, because they were unique to me. My relationship with my mum, being the only daughter she had, was unique to me and her, and that caused the aloneness. I remember walking behind the coffin as it was carried into the church, and it felt as if it were not me. For some reason I thought, *If this was really mum's funeral, my brothers would be here*. I would not be doing this on my own. I would not have to make all the decisions, without knowing if I was making the right ones. So yes, I was going through the motions with a heavy heart. There was also a part of me that was disappointed with my aunt because she did not come over. I thought if anyone could have come, it would have been her, as she had the means. I knew I was being unreasonable, but I could not help it. I had even offered to pay for the ticket, as family and friends from both near and far had been very generous in giving monetary gifts towards the funeral planning. For some time afterward I held it against her that she did not make it for the funeral. It took me a while to forgive her for not coming. Not that she could have come, but in my grief I was not considering all the challenges and obstacles that prevented her travelling to England.

The service was lovely just as Mum would have wanted. There were quite a lot of people there, including Trevor's sister and her husband. I was really touched, as they had not even met my mum, but they had heard a lot about her from Trevor. There was also family from London who attended the funeral. Afterward, we had a repast at a local restaurant. The whole day was a bit of a blur for me. It was a very sad and emotional event and emotionally exhausting for me.

Since Mum had not wanted to be taken back to Sierra Leone, I had paid for her to be buried in a plot at the local cemetery. She had said at the time that, since I had met Trevor, she saw my future to be in England, not in Sierra Leone. So, she wanted to be buried here, where I would always be near to her place of rest and able to visit and lay flowers on her grave. I agreed with her, as at that time it would have been a very serious logistic issue to take her body to Sierra Leone.

After the funeral I had to navigate a new normal without my mum. I could not stay in the flat, as there were too many memories, both good and bad, which were making me really sad. Also, without her income I could not afford to keep it on my own. I had decided I would look for a one-bedroom flat or studio that I could afford with the salary from the two part-time jobs I had. I was still at university and could not work full time even if I wanted to, as I was on a student's visa.

Fortunately, it was easy to find another flat that would be suitable for me. It was still very close to the town centre and all the places I frequented. I was able to put down a deposit, give notice to the landlord of the flat we had been renting, and then get back the deposit Mum had put down, which came in handy. It was quite an emotional experience packing up to move out of the flat. Mum had acquired a lot of stuff before she became ill. There were things she had planned to ship over to Sierra Leone for my brothers and her grandchildren. I had no clue that she had so much stuff, including clothes, shoes, household items, and educational material. I could have opened a bric-a-brac shop with all the stuff I had to put into storage, as I could not bear to give it away at that time. There was no way I could move everything we had in the two-bedroom flat into a one-bedroom flat. Trevor suggested storing some of the stuff that I did not need immediately at his parents' house, as they had an outside shed with space for storage. I was grateful for this alternative.

My new place was in a shared house but was self-contained with my own kitchen and bathroom. I only shared the main entrance into the house. It was a massive house that had been converted into self-contained flats, and it suited my needs. It was also less than ten minutes' walk from the flat where Mum and I had lived. I was fortunate to have found it, as I did not have to change my route to work or to the university. It was the same route, just from a different starting point.

I loved my flat. It was the first time I had ever had a place of my own. I had always lived with someone, so it was great to experience being fully independent. I was in my early thirties and this was the first time I was living on my own. I could decorate and furnish the place the way I liked it, according to my own taste. My mum loved little ornaments and stuff. I did not mind them, but I wanted my space to be a bit minimalistic, not too crowded. It was great to be able to put my stamp on the place and show my personality.

I was not there for long. This was my new home for only six months, as Trevor and I got married exactly six months after my mum passed. I had not seen that in my immediate future, but God works in mysterious ways.

12

DIFFERENT LOSSES: HOW DO THEY COMPARE?

The loss of my mum was very hard, as I missed her terribly. We had been a unit since I had arrived in England. The loss I felt was different from the loss of my brother Frank. The pain was different and the healing was different. This is something very important for those who have never experienced loss of a close loved one before to know. If you are supporting a person who has lost someone dear to them, don't make comparisons between experiences. All deaths are experienced differently. The journey and pace will be different.

When I lost my brother, I experienced very different emotions compared to what I experienced when I lost my mum. I felt alone when I lost mum because my brothers and other close family were in Sierra Leone. When I lost my brother, I was in Sierra Leone with my other brothers and close family, but Mum was in England, so the emotions were different.

I lost my dad before I lost my brother and my mum. I would say that was the first significant loss I experienced before my brother. The difficulty in that loss was that I felt I had not gotten to know him as well as I could have.

My mum and dad were not married, so I never got to know my dad as well as I would have liked because I never lived with him.

The short visits with my dad at his house were very superficial in a way. I was always on my best behaviour, so he did not get to see the real me. He was very much old-school, very focused on education. He put a lot of emphasis on working hard at school and university to attain good results. He drilled into my brother and me that that was all he could give us, a good education. But no one could take that away from us. I don't disagree with him, but I also think that part of an education is also being taught important life skills. These I had to depend on my mum for.

I got to know my dad a bit more when I was able to visit him in his office. If I was showing him good results from school, it would put him in a good mood. Then we could chat about other stuff; it wouldn't just be him scolding me like he did if I brought bad results from school. I also felt in those days that my visits were always centred around something I needed, rather than visiting him simply because he was my dad. At the time it seemed to me like a waste to spend all that money on transportation if I was not also combining the effort with a request for something I needed for school or for home. When I reflect on it now, I do feel bad. But unfortunately, as a child with parents living in two different locations, I had to make it work.

My last few visits to him had been because I had been chosen by one of my cousins to be one of the chief bridesmaids at her wedding. I was really excited, as it was the first time I had been asked, so it would be my first time as part of a bridal party. I needed shoes and fabric to make the dress.

In those days people hardly went to a shop to get ready-made outfits, and I had already learnt how to make dresses from mum, as she was very good with the sewing machine. All I really needed was the fabric to make the outfit for the wedding.

My dad was very interested in the role I would be playing as a chief bridesmaid. We used to discuss what was required and how I would make sure that the bride had a good day. I never thought that he would pass before the wedding took place. But a week or so before the wedding, he was admitted to the hospital for something that at first was minor but then became very serious.

My brother and I visited him at the hospital, as it was walking distance from where we lived. In the short conversation that we had, he quoted *Macbeth*: "If it were done when 'tis done, then 'twere well / It were done quickly" (1.7.1). This is very similar to what Jesus says to Judas in the Bible: "What you are going to do, do quickly [without delay]" (John 13:27). This has stuck with my brother and me all these years, because that was the last thing he said to us before he passed.

The next day when we were informed that he had passed, we could not believe it. Even though we were not very close, it was still hard. With the loss of my dad, I mourned the missed opportunities to get to know him as a person, to learn what he liked apart from his love for good education. I mourned that I did not get to know what his favourite colour or his favourite food were, as my time with him had been so functional. It was mostly about schoolwork, doing well in school to achieve qualifications. He was very disciplined and to some extent, I was always afraid of putting my foot wrong, which meant that I did not get to know him as well as I would have liked.

I remember when I got to puberty and started noticing boys. Mum had caught me reading romances published by Mills & Boon and a Caroline Courtney regency romance book. I had moved on from my Enid Blyton children's books and she was concerned. She told my dad, who thought the best thing would be to get me a book that would educate me on everything a teenage girl should know. He actually bought a book called *Everything a Teenage Girl Should Know*, written by Dr. John F. Knight. I got more than I bargained for with that book. My suggestion to any mums and dads out there is to make sure you have read the book in question before giving it to your children, especially if they are in the early stages of puberty. My mum and dad were very traditional and very uncomfortable talking about the "birds and the bees," so it was either having a stuttering and embarrassing conversation or giving me a book that perhaps said a lot more than they wanted to say.

Though I was not as close to my dad as I was to my mum, his passing was still a great loss to me. As I was much younger at the time, the responsibility of arranging the funeral was left to my dad's siblings and to my own older siblings. They did all the planning, and I just did what I was told, which was mainly going with them to different places as the funeral arrangements came together.

Another loss that I experienced after my mum was my maternal grandmother. I was close with my grandmother, so when I first came to England, she was one of the people I missed a lot. I had spent some of my early years with her when my mum had gone to study in England. For about two years, we lived with my grandmother and my aunt (the one who later brought me to England). In those days she was very strong and would manage the home so that my aunt could focus on being the high-powered obstetrician and gynaecologist that she was. My grandmother used to look after chickens, ducks, and goats, as we were not in the city but in a smaller town outside the capital. At that early age we had the responsibility of feeding the chickens in the morning and evening. I loved the baby chicks and the baby ducklings, and I remember chasing after the chickens if they escaped from the coop. This is probably one of the reasons I really loved the children's movie *Chicken Run*, which I used to love watching with my children when they were younger.

I had continued to spend a lot of time with my grandmother, even after I was no longer living with her. I would visit her religiously every two weeks to do her hair. She loved having her scalp moisturised, as she said it was like receiving a head massage. She would nod off to sleep, so I would be gentle while doing her hair in order not to wake her up. She also taught me how to mark canvass with wool to make carpet slippers, which was the customary footwear to be worn with a traditional Krio outfit.

It was really sad when she passed, especially as I was in England and could not attend the funeral. But she had lived a long and happy life and died at ninety-five years old.

13

MARLEY, ALWAYS IN MY HEART

I would like to say that all these different losses I had gone through had prepared me for the hardest loss I was yet to face, but I would be telling a lie. I don't believe that previous losses can prepare you for the next loss you encounter, as all losses are different and, depending on the circumstances, subsequent losses could be even harder to endure than the previous ones. This was the case with my youngest son, who I lost to death by suicide. If you don't know the background to this story, then I recommend reading my book *Marley's Memoir: The Journey to an Irreversible Action and the Aftermath*.

It is now coming up on four years since I lost my youngest son Marley just a week after his eighteenth birthday. Some days it feels like yesterday. On other days, I feel like it happened longer than four years ago.

I still struggle with meeting new people who don't know my story. I dread when the inevitable questions come up, *Do you have any children? How many children have you got?* But I was really encouraged recently when I met someone in church for the first time who had a six-month-old baby. Even before I could ask her about her baby, she told me she had five children. In my heart I was thinking, *Wow, she must have her hands full*, as I reckoned the oldest would not be more than ten years old. She then went on to say that two of the children were in heaven because they had passed—one was a miscarriage and the other was when they were a baby. But she said she always told people that she has five children, it's just that two of them have gone ahead to heaven. I was amazed at her strength and her perspective. I thought I should not shy away from telling people that I have two sons and one has already gone ahead to heaven.

I still talk to God about Marley, asking if there could have been another way. You would think that, after so much time has passed, I would no longer be asking God these kind of questions. But when I think about it, I do feel that I still need that reassurance from God that there was no other way. God is so faithful; He doesn't chastise me for still asking the same question when the deed has already been done. He shows that He cares. He shows that He loves me by reaffirming that there was no other way. He also reminds me that I will not understand everything in this life.

One of the ways He reassures me is by bringing other young people to my attention, young people whose mental health issues have worsened and have even gone on to harm not just themselves but others as well. These actions cause pain and loss for multiple sets of parents, for the parents of the young person with mental health struggles and for the parents whose loved ones were harmed. I have no way of knowing if this could have been our situation as well. But I think back on Marley's lack of response to talk therapy, and I consider that, from the time he finished school to when he ended his life, his mental health had been deteriorating into paranoia, imagining what people were saying and thinking. I can only guess that it might have worsened to the point where he could have harmed someone else. I have to thank God that it did not get to that point.

Since Marley's passing, the foundation that I set up as his legacy, Marley's Aart Foundation, has been providing funding for art therapy for children with mental health conditions. We started working with a local organisation that supports children with emotional and mental health issues, including trauma and bereavement conditions, and we are now working closely with Marley's secondary school. Since we started funding the art therapy at the school, we have made a difference in the mental well-being of over twenty-five different children. The foundation has given me a purpose, knowing I can make a difference for other children and young people who are struggling with their mental health like Marley was. At a recent meeting with the school, it was rewarding to hear the impact of what we are doing through the foundation. At present the foundation funds two individual art therapy sessions once a week and two group therapy sessions once a week for children ranging in age from eleven to sixteen. Some of the children, especially the eleven-year-olds who are new to the school, have found the new school environment much more challenging than their previous schools, especially if they are naturally introverted. They have the tendency to be anxious and have difficulties in social environments meeting new people and making connections. The art therapy really helped them to express themselves and provide mechanisms to help them navigate this phase. This particular age group, transitioning from primary to secondary school, is very dear to me, as it was at this stage that I started noticing a difference in Marley, which at the time I did not understand. I had at first just put it down to the change of school. Now I strongly believe that the earlier the child gets help, the better the response to the therapy will be. I am also very supportive of the children who are suffering from exam anxiety and feeling the pressure to get good grades in order to take their next step in their education. I was especially happy to hear that a number of girls who had suffered with anxiety and missed a lot of school because of it had eventually pushed through to take their GCSEs after they had had group art therapy. It was rewarding to know that Marley's Aart Foundation has helped even in a small way.

I look to God every day as I trust in His plan for the foundation. I am told all the time how God would enlarge the foundation to be national and even international because it is doing such important work. At this moment I am taking it one step at a time, trusting in God for His guidance. If God wants it to stay as it is, just supporting the children in Bedfordshire, then I am happy to be doing that. If He wants it to grow to become national and international, then He will make a way and a provision for that.

Sometimes I am lost in my own world, thinking about Marley and what he would have been doing if he were here. Eight months ago, on the day before he would have turned twenty-one, we held the third Marley's 8KM Memory Walk, a fundraising event that we have been doing since the first anniversary of his passing. This time we had a higher number of supporters than in any of the previous years. It was a very cold, freezing morning, so I was expecting that some of the people who had said they would do the walk might pull out. But as with the previous year, everyone turned out in record numbers to do the five-mile walk. When we reached the end point, I thanked everyone and shared that the next day would have been Marley's twenty-first birthday.

I was in two minds whether to go to church that day or not. In the end I went. I felt I had to push through, because God is with me. When I got to church, I became overwhelmed with what could have been. I allowed myself to imagine what Marley could have looked like. He was a handsome young man, and I think he would probably have filled out into an adult with facial hair. He was also taller than his brother, and I imagined both of them together. It was hard that I had been denied the experience of seeing them like that because he passed so young. I allowed the tears to fall as I sat in church before the service started. A sister who I regularly pray with came over and put her hands around me. She had been sitting behind me, so she must have been prompted by God. Because my tears were silent, she could not hear me or see me, but I leaned into the comfort she was offering. It was hard that I had been robbed of seeing him at twenty-one. After this I felt better. I realised that it had been a while since I had cried over losing Marley. It's not that I don't want to cry or that I hold it in, far from it. In those early days I cried so much that I think I might have run out of physical tears.

I realised that every milestone would be hard for me. When it comes to the years when he would have been twenty-five, thirty, and so forth, I will probably get very emotional. Later I also realised that it's not just his milestones that get me emotional; I am also affected by other children who were born the same year as or the year after him. Each time I celebrate another young person's twenty-first birthday, it will be bittersweet. I would look at Marley's photos from when he was at eighteen and imagine how he would have looked at twenty-one. Would he still be suffering from mental health issues? Would he have become the animator that he wanted to be? These are all unanswered questions that I will not know the answer to in this life. It will always feel like he passed too soon, even though I am slowly accepting that nothing happens too soon in God's timing. The way I feel today, I don't think I will ever accept it. I will always have those questions, whether it is four years or twenty years later.

When I lost my mum, I thought that, after I got married and after I had Nathan and Marley, I would not miss her with the same intensity that I did previously. How wrong I was. Each milestone in my life would remind me of what it would have been like if Mum had been there—to see my children, for my children to know their grandmother, to observe how loving she would have been with them, probably spoiling them by letting them get away with stuff I would not have allowed. The love I have for my mother is a different kind of love compared to the love I have for Marley, and therefore the grief over their losses has been different. Yet the similarity is that they are not here for any future milestones.

Twenty years after my mum passed, I remember waking up one morning and being gripped by a sudden yearning for her voice and touch. That feeling stayed with me for almost the whole day. By the evening, I was sobbing uncontrollably and Trevor and the children were asking me what was wrong. I was so choked up with emotion, I could barely speak. I was finally able to tell them that I missed my mum. Of course, they could not understand what that felt like, because neither Trevor nor the children had lost anyone so close to them. All they could do was give me a hug. Now I know that, after losing Marley, I will not be surprised if ten or twenty years from now, I will get overwhelmed with emotions as if it had just happened. It is the way we are made. Our God cares and weeps over us when we stray from Him and rejoices when we come back to Him. We are made in His image and likeness, as it says in the Bible:

> "So, God created man in His own image, in the image *and* likeness of God He created him; male and female He created them."
>
> (Genesis 1:27)

It should not come as a surprise to us that we care so much because we are only imitating God our Father.

14

Final Words

The message from my pastor on 29 December 2020 at the service for my son Marley will always stay with me. He voiced what most of us had been thinking or even saying out aloud: Why do bad things happen? Why did this happen? Why would God allow someone who was so young to end their life? He encouraged us to say we do not know why bad things happen. Especially as believers, we may feel we are expected to have all the answers, but we do not have all the answers. We cannot know and we should not try to give an answer to the question of why bad things happen because there are certain things we would not understand or otherwise have the answers for in this life.

We are never ready to lose a loved one. It does not matter how old they are or how sick they are. We may think we are ready if we have walked the journey with that loved one through their illness. But there is something about parting with someone that nothing can prepare you for. When they finally leave this world and we realise that we will never again be able to speak with and interact with that person as before, the reality hits us. We are filled with insurmountable pain and loss.

It has been the same for everyone close to me that I lost. But of all the losses, the three very significant ones are my brother Frank, my mum, and Marley. My dad and the other brothers and relations I have lost have been painful but not as much as these three for the reasons I have shared in the previous chapters. At the church on that horrible day at the service for my son Marley, my pastor told us that, in each situation, God cares. He said that he knows without a doubt that God cares. He cares what happened to Frank, to my mum, and to Marley. He knew how each of these situations would impact me and my future. He went on to quote the following verse from the Bible:

> "The Lord is near to the heartbroken And He saves those who are crushed in spirit (contrite in heart, truly sorry for their sin)."
>
> (Psalm 34:18)

When we are heartbroken, we may not feel like or think that God is near, but He is. He is the one who helps us to put one foot in front of the other to take one step and another. If it were not for Him, I would not be here. The pain I felt at losing Marley so unexpectedly and suddenly no one could understand. Only God knows. God cares deeply about what happens to us. He knew exactly what Frank was going through; He knew exactly what my mum was going through; and He knew exactly what Marley was going through. He had compassion for their struggles, and because He cares, He allowed them to leave this world. For us it was very painful parting from them. But for those who have left, they were now without any pain.

Each parting also birthed something new. When I lost my brother, it opened the door for me to travel to a new life in England with my mum. I do not know if my aunt would have been moved to purchase a ticket for me to visit my mum if the loss of my brother had not triggered it.

When I lost my mum, it opened the door for me to get married and start a new chapter in my life as a wife and later as a mother. I am not saying that if my mum had not passed I would not have got married. I had of course already met Trevor before my mum passed. What I am saying is that being on my own and experiencing the character development that took place during that time of loss enabled me to move into another level of maturity that served me during the challenges of marriage.

The passing of my son Marley has also opened a door and taken me to another level of maturity. I had never seen myself being an activist. I was more of an advocate—let someone else take the lead and I would be there to support them. With the founding of Marley's Aart Foundation, I have found myself at the front, leading the way with others supporting me in the background. Yes, I have held positions in my career that enabled me to take the lead in several situations, but at the end of the day, there was always someone in front of me. My manager or my manager's manager would be there to act as a cushion to fall back on. I certainly could not push something through if they were not happy with it. In my current role as founder of Marley's Aart Foundation, I have a very strong team of trustees, but they look to me to lead from the front. The unique vision

I was given came to me through the pain I experienced then and still experience now any time I meet someone who would be the same age as Marley. The motivation I have to help support children and young people is unique to me. Not that others, especially the trustees, don't have the same motivation, but theirs is coming from a different place than mine. As a mother who lost her son to suicide, I have this burden to help other children in my own small way through the foundation. If the art therapy that the foundation funds prevent one child from taking their life, then my goal is complete. If a mother who has been through similar trauma of losing their child by suicide is comforted by reading about my experience, or if that mother is comforted to find that God cares not just for me but for each and every one of us, and if that mother discovers that because I could be strong then she can be strong as well, then I am satisfied that I have accomplished something.

As I come to the end of this book series on grief and loss, I would like to share that it has been therapeutic for me to write them. Sometimes I have felt very exposed, as I am capturing my raw emotions for others to read and I am sharing about what I have gone through and I am still going through since losing Marley. But I could not be anything other than my authentic self. Though it has been therapeutic, it has also been hard to bring some of these memories back to the forefront of my mind. I had buried the memory of some of these sad events that I had gone through. After writing about it, though, I feel lighter, better than I did before. It has been worth it. Writing has also helped me to see things in a better perspective, a much more mature perspective than I had at the time when some of these events took place. I have been able to reflect on these events and gain more clarity and acceptance. This process has helped me to dig deep into things that I had buried in my heart, but it has been good to resurrect those memories and understand a bit better how I felt at the time. I believe by doing this, I have been able to release those memories and feelings and be better for it.

I would hope that others who read my books would be encouraged to move forward, not without their loved ones but with the capacity to keep them in their hearts, as they will always be part of us. I have learnt that it is important to have some coping mechanisms in place to help you get through each day, week, month, and year.

I regularly meet with friends for coffee, lunch, or dinner. It is one of the things that keeps me going. I have also become very active in my church since I took voluntary redundancy from my previous employer of eighteen years. I am part of the church's Bereavement Support team, as I want to be able to help others, just as another local bereavement group helped me when I first lost Marley. I can share with others what was beneficial for me and what was not. Hopefully some of this information can be useful to others. I share a lot about my grieving process in my second book, *Living Without Marley*.

Just as I have had the opportunity to listen to others in similar situations, I have also read books by others sharing the story of how they pulled through their loss. I have also prayed with some and just spent time with others as they navigate their grief. Helping others by simply walking beside them as they navigate their grief journey can be very helpful. It counteracts that innate helplessness that all of us feel when we lose someone. You feel like there is something you could have done to prevent them from passing, which of course, in most or all cases, there isn't.

I try to plan different things to look forward to. That is one of the many coping mechanisms that I took from my first bereavement support group. I plan regular spa days or outings to the theatre to see a play or hear a musical concert. Sometimes it's something as effortless as joining the ladies in church for Saturday morning walks. When I can, I also travel, visiting family and friends in different countries. Last year I went to Stockholm in Sweden with two of my close friends. I had been to Stockholm a lot previously though each time it was for business, never for leisure. It was good to go as a tourist and to take time to see all the landmarks. This year I also visited Krakow in Poland, another country that I had been to a lot for business but never for pleasure. It was great to be able to take in all the rich history of Krakow with my own very personal guide, my friend Joanna.

I don't know what the future holds, but I definitely will embrace it as I have done in the past and the present. I would like to continue helping children and young people with mental health conditions, and I would like to continue giving support to parents and caregivers who are going through grief and loss similar to mine. I would also like to continue to share my experiences with others if it would give them strength, comfort, and hope.

I am a Christian believer, and I could not write this book without sharing about the goodness of God. Despite everything that I have experienced, I believe in God. Even with all the other coping mechanisms that I have, without God I would not be strong. If you are of a different faith, I applaud you and encourage you to open your heart and let God speak to you. If you have no faith at all, try to keep an open heart for God to speak to you.

Lastly, I would like to let you know that no matter what you may have gone through or are currently going through, He cares. God cares for you. He cares about the little things that upset you the same way He cares about the big things that upset you. He promises to never abandon us. As it says in Deuteronomy 31:8:

> "It is the Lord who goes before you; He will be with you. He will not fail you or abandon you. Do not fear or be dismayed."

Trust Him because He cares.

15: Epilogue

Three Years & Nine Months Later

Today is my fourth birthday without Marley. As I said in the last chapter, I always plan to spend my birthday in a meaningful way as I celebrate the day I was born and will continue to do so every year. Most birthdays have been small but meaningful celebrations whilst for significant milestones, there have been bigger celebrations.

Today my plan was to spend the day with one of my close friends in London, having a makeover and a photo shoot. The itinerary had been planned, the train tickets bought, and the pickup time agreed upon. We drove to the train station with plenty of time to get a parking ticket and make our way to the platform. But I happened to look towards the barriers and saw a small group of people talking to the station attendants. I pointed this out to my friend as she was busy purchasing the parking ticket with her phone. She asked me to go ahead and see what was going on.

I was not expecting to suddenly be thrown back to the traumatic loss of Marley. The station attendant had closed the barriers so no one could get through with their train tickets because someone had jumped onto the track and been hit by a fast-moving train. This had happened about a few miles before our station. All trains were cancelled for the foreseeable future. I looked across to the other side of the station and saw a group of police officers and paramedics. It was like flashback to December 2020 when I had had to call the paramedics for Marley.

I was really distraught. My empathy kicked in as I started thinking of this person and the family and friends who would be receiving the sad and traumatic news that their loved one had ended their life. I became quite emotional because it was the last thing I expected to happen on my birthday. With the train cancelled, we had to find another way of getting to London.

We succeeded in getting an Uber for a very reasonable price, and whilst we were in the Uber on our way to London, I called the studio to let them know that we might not make our appointment. They were very understanding and advised us to let them know if we would be delayed for more than five minutes once we got to London, so that they could reschedule us for an hour later at no additional charge. In the midst of this sad situation I asked God, Why did this happen? Why did this person feel so low that they thought they could not last another week, even another day, and had to end their life? "God cares" was what was being impressed in my heart.

I want to appeal to anyone who has suicidal thoughts or experiences low moods or feelings of worthlessness: ending your life is not the answer. In some ways it transfers a burden to your loved ones. The impact of your action will stay with your family and friends forever. It is irreversible and there is no do over. Your family and friends will have to live with this burden for the rest of their lives. And as it happened with me, they might relive the whole traumatic experience again and again if they know of someone else who has lost their life by suicide. The answer to suicidal thoughts, low moods, and feelings of worthlessness is to get help. Speak to your family or to a close friend and let them support you through your difficult times.

I thank God that, because He cares and is a loving God, I went on to enjoy the rest of my birthday. But there was certainly that part of me that continued to grieve for another life lost by suicide.

Please reach out to any organisations that can help and support you if you do not want to speak to your friends or family.

ABOUT THE AUTHOR

Majendi Jarrett is a Christian author and speaker. She is the author of *Marley's Memoir: The Journey to an Irreversible Action and the Aftermath*, *Living Without Marley*, and *He Cares*. She often speaks at churches, schools, and corporate events. She is a graduate of Fourah Bay College in Freetown, Sierra Leone, and the University of Bedfordshire in the United Kingdom. She started writing in 2019 and published her first book in 2022, with a focus on real-life experiences. She currently lives in Bedfordshire with her husband, son, and a pond of tropical fish.

www.ingramcontent.com/pod-product-compliance
Lightning Source LLC
Chambersburg PA
CBHW020416010526
44118CB00010B/276